Stowe
THE PEOPLE AND THE PLACE

Michael Bevington

with
George Clarke,
Jonathan Marsden
and Tim Knox

First published in 2011 by
The National Trust
Heelis
Kemble Drive
Swindon SN2 2NA

In association with
Scala Publishers Ltd
Northburgh House
10 Northburgh Street
London EC1V 0AT
www.scalapublishers.com

ISBN 978-0-70780-417-0

Text edited by Oliver Garnett
Project managed by Jessica Hodge
Designed by Isambard Thomas
Printed in Spain

10 9 8 7 6 5 4 3 2 1

Frontispiece:
The Temple of Venus

Front cover:
The Oxford Bridge and Boycott Pavilion

Back cover:
The Corinthan Arch frames a spectacular
view of the south front of the house

ACKNOWLEDGEMENTS

Bodleian Library, Oxford: p.27 *below*
Bridgeman Art Library/Musée Carnavalet, Paris: p.86
Buckingham County Museum: pp59, 79 *top*
Huntington Library, California: p.21
Mary Evans Picture Library: p.66
National Gallery of Ireland: p.55
National Gallery of Victoria, Melbourne: p.41
National Portrait Gallery, London: pp11, 28 *both*, 36, 61
National Trust/Paul Watson: front cover, back cover, pp7, 10 *below*,
    13 top, 14, 15, 25, 29, 30, 31 *both*, 32, 34-5, 38, 39, 42, 46-7, 48, 50
    below, 51 *below*, 52, 53, 56, 57, 60, 65, 67, 74 *both*, 75, 76, 77, 78, 79
    below, 81, 85
National Trust Images/Andrew Butler: pp1-2, 8-9, 12, 58,
NT Images/Mike Caldwell: p.71
NT Images/Rod Edwards: pp18-19, 50-1 *top*, 69
NT Images/John Hammond: pp24, 82-3
NT Images/ Jerry Harpur: pp10 top, 13 *bottom*, 70 *top*
NT Images/Angelo Hornak: pp43
NT Images/James Mortimer: p.70 *below*
NT Images/Rupert Truman: pp33, 37, 49, 72-3
NT Images/Mike Williams: p.84
Private Collection/photo © Christie's Images/The Bridgeman Art Library
    CH 19870: p.26
Royal Commission on the Historical Monuments of England: pp22-3
Stowe School: pp17, 63, 64
Vancouver Art Gallery, Founders' Fund: p.27 *top*

I

The meaning of Stowe

Visitors to Stowe sometimes ask, understandably enough, where the flower gardens are, and it has to be explained that Stowe is not that kind of garden. Though there are a few formal flowerbeds within the balustrade on the south side of the house, all beyond is a picture of idealised nature, whose elements are grass and trees and water, with buildings carefully sited to give accents to the view and allow the wandering eye a resting place. An equally important question is 'What does the garden mean?' But that is a question which visitors hardly ever ask, for the concept that a garden as large as Stowe could have a specific and detailed programme of meaning – a sort of philosophic or political manifesto on the ground – is alien to our way of thinking. Yet it has been a controlling principle in some of the great gardens of the past. The Roman emperor Hadrian followed it at Tivoli. So did the creators of several gardens in Renaissance Italy, and the idea was taken up in eighteenth-century England, at Stourhead in Wiltshire, for example. Nowhere, however, was the garden programme more elaborate and detailed than at Stowe.

The family who created it were eighteenth-century Whigs, conscious descendants of the men whose opposition to the absolutist ambitions of the Stuart monarchy in the previous century had culminated in the Glorious Revolution of 1688. As a result, they could claim to have established constitutional monarchy and political freedom in England, and they saw themselves as the chosen defenders of liberty. Throughout the eighteenth century, the proprietors of Stowe and their relations were steadfast, if independent, adherents to the Whig cause, even to their own political disadvantage, and, as John Martin Robinson remarks, this allegiance 'runs through the garden architecture like a leitmotif'.[1]

Sir Richard Temple served gallantly under the Duke of Marlborough in the war of the Spanish succession, which ended in 1713, and was created baron in 1714 and Viscount Cobham in 1718.

Woden, one of the Saxon Deities installed by Lord Cobham

The Palladian Bridge was
decorated with sculptural
reliefs stressing the
importance of trade to
British prosperity

He returned home to Stowe and began to lay out formal gardens, in which the walks and cross-walks were terminated by buildings and monuments, with all the conventional garden furniture. Early on, he demonstrated his loyalty to the new, and still none too secure, Hanoverian regime by setting up an equestrian statue of George I, and this was followed by statues of the Prince and Princess of Wales (later George II and Queen Caroline), a special compliment being paid to Caroline, whose statue was sited directly facing that of Venus in the Rotondo, so that princess and goddess seemed to gaze at each other as equals. This can perhaps be seen as mere political flattery but, as the gardens departed from strict symmetry, expanding southwards and westwards during the 1720s to embrace Home Park within a perimeter walk, an astonishing variety of idiosyncratic and evocative buildings was added: a temple of honour surrounded by the busts of eight British 'worthies'; a miniature villa in the latest Palladian taste; statues of the seven Saxon gods who gave their names to the days of the week; a memorial pyramid to Cobham's friend, the architect and dramatist Sir John Vanbrugh, who designed several of these buildings; a hermitage with a 'ruined' turret; and so on. These were described

[left]
**The statue of George I
was intended to
demonstrate Cobham's
loyalty to the new
Hanoverian regime**

[below left]
**The statue of Venus, in
the Rotondo designed by
Cobham's friend Sir John
Vanbrugh**

[below]
**William Kent, who
designed the Elysian
Fields, painted by
William Aikman,
*c.*1723–25**

in the topographical poem *Stowe* by Gilbert West, Cobham's nephew, published in 1732, and it is clear from the poem that until that date, though the physical layout of the garden followed an artistic design, the ideas had been added piecemeal, as an afterthought and in no coherent order. From 1733, however, when a new area on the eastern side was taken into the garden to form the Elysian Fields, the programme of ideas was conceived as an organic part of the whole. The British Worthies, for example, were brought across into the Elysian Fields, not only as a focus of the pictorial design but also as a key piece in the iconographical theme.

The origin of the new garden was almost certainly an essay by Joseph Addison in *The Tatler* (No. 123, 21 January 1710), describing an allegorical dream. After falling asleep, Addison relates that he found himself in a huge wood, which had many paths and was full of people. He joined a group of middle-aged men marching 'behind the standard of Ambition', and describes the route he took and the buildings he saw. The essential features of the Elysian Fields are all there: a long straight path (the Great Cross Walk at Stowe) was terminated by a temple of virtue (Ancient Virtue), beyond which (over the river) lay a temple of honour (British Worthies); nearby was a ruinous temple of vanity (Modern Virtue). The classes of people mentioned in the dream, and the effigies too, correspond to the statues actually set up in the gardens. It therefore seems beyond doubt that Addison's essay provided the overall programme to be illustrated by the architect and garden designer. By 1733 William Kent was acting in both these capacities at Stowe, and so the decorative buildings and the garden setting must have come from his hand. But the iconography would have been worked out by Gilbert West and the other literary members of Cobham's circle. Very likely Alexander Pope, himself an enthusiastic gardener and frequent house-guest at Stowe, had a share in it. When they came to select heroic figures for the Temple of Ancient Virtue, it was to Greece they turned rather than Rome, for the record of imperial Roman tyranny recalled French and Stuart despotism too strongly. Homer, Socrates and Epaminondas were there as, respectively, the greatest poet, philosopher and soldier of the Ancient World; all three had been chosen by Pope in 1711 to fill the same positions in his poem *The Temple of Fame*. The fourth was the law-giver Lycurgus, who was believed to have established in Sparta the balanced constitution of limited monarchy so much admired by eighteenth-century Whigs.

The same theme was continued on the other side of the valley in the Temple of British Worthies, which contained the 16 members of the British nation regarded by Cobham's circle as worthy to be seen in the same company. The eight men of contemplation included poets, scientists and philosophers such as Shakespeare, Milton, Newton and

Locke, all 'thinkers' revered by the Whig establishment. Locke in particular was a Whig hero, providing in his *Second Treatise of Government* (1690) the philosophic justification for the Glorious Revolution. The eight men of action were mostly statesmen and soldiers from recent English history, heroes who had fought, and in some cases died, in the struggle against the Stuarts; men like Sir Walter Ralegh and John Hampden, and, most importantly, William III. From their situation beside the stream the British Worthies looked up – literally and metaphorically – at their heroic Greek exemplars in the Temple of Ancient Virtue, who were thus offered as models for any contemporary Englishman ambitious to serve his country.

All these features were in accord with an ideal Whig vision of government. But in 1733, between the conception of the programme

The Temple of Friendship

[above]
Bust of the philosopher John Locke, in the Temple of British Worthies

[left]
The Temple of British Worthies celebrates figures of thought and action revered by the Whigs

and its detailed execution, Cobham fell out with the prime minister, Sir Robert Walpole, over the Excise Bill, was dismissed from his regiment, and joined other prominent Whigs in opposition. The political platform of these self-styled 'Patriots' was the traditional Whig defence of liberty and the constitution, which, they claimed, were being cynically destroyed by Walpole's policy of systematic corruption in Parliament. Their campaign was concentrated against Walpole himself, but by implication, though it could only be hinted at, they were also opposing George II. They took as their figurehead Frederick, Prince of Wales, who had quarrelled with his father and set up an independent court, and before long another of Cobham's nephews, George Lyttelton, became the Prince's secretary. So in the gardens of Stowe, now a hotbed of Patriot opposition, the simple philosophic statement was overlaid with a political manifesto.

This shift in Cobham's political position explains the selection of the only two Worthies from earlier English history, King Alfred and Edward, Prince of Wales, better known to us as the Black Prince. Alfred, who, according to his inscription, 'crush'd corruption, guarded liberty, and was the founder of the English constitution', embodied the same theme as Lycurgus. But he was also there, no less importantly, as an ironic statement of everything that George II was not. And Edward, Prince of Wales was a thin disguise for Frederick, who the Patriots hoped would take Alfred rather than George as his model when he became king, and would 'preserve his natural gentleness and modesty … in the height of glory and fortune', like the Black Prince. Inscriptions above other Worthies contained similar messages, inviting the viewer to read between the lines, but the most obvious - and curious - item of this Patriot manifesto was the adaptation of Addison's temple of vanity. The Temple of Ancient Virtue, with its four heroic figures from Greek Antiquity, was described in Benton Seeley's 1744 guide to Stowe as being 'in a very flourishing condition', in contrast with the Temple of Modern Virtue nearby, which was built as a ruin, with a headless statue inside, as a satirical comment on the degraded state of contemporary public life.

After Frederick had paid an ostentatious visit to Stowe in 1737, the political theme became more explicit. Next to be developed was

Hawkwell Field, the eastern area of the garden, and the Temple of Friendship was built at its southern end to house ten busts of the Patriots, now quite openly including Frederick. On the ceiling was an allegorical picture of Britannia, with three additional figures bearing scrolls; two of the scrolls proudly recorded British achievements in the reigns of Edward III and Elizabeth, whereas the name on the third – presumed to be George II – was 'cover'd with her Mantle' in shame, in Seeley's description. This was an attack on what the Patriots saw as Walpole's weak foreign policy, jeopardising Britain's trade. The Palladian Bridge nearby (built with a blank wall on its eastern side, which was not visible from the house) further illustrated the mercantile theme of Whig policy. Paintings of Ralegh and William Penn, two of Britain's colonial pioneers, were placed at either end, and between them was a sculpted relief of the four continents bringing their products to Britannia, a demonstration of the close links between Whig politicians

The Gothic Temple dominated Hawkwell Field and formed the climax of Cobham's political agenda

Sculpture of Sunna; Cobham moved the seven Saxon Deities from their original positions to surround the Gothic Temple

and City merchants. At the northern end of the vista stood the Queen's Temple, the domain of Lady Cobham, decorated with murals of ladies employed in shellwork and other pursuits regarded as appropriate to their sex – and not meddling, as Queen Caroline had, in politics, which should be the business of men. Set high on the hill between the Queen's Temple and the Temple of Friendship, and thus visible from many corners of the estate, was the Gothic Temple, the climax of Cobham's political gardening.

'Gothic' conveys little more to us now than an architectural style, but to the eighteenth century it was, like 'Goth', a word of potent meaning. Assumed to be synonymous with 'Germanic' (as 'Goth' was with 'Jute'), it suggested the vigour, hardihood and love of liberty of those tough northern tribes who conquered Rome, in contrast with the perceived spineless servility of the Latin peoples. The democratic procedures which the Roman historian Tacitus had described as typical of Germanic assemblies were, in the eighteenth century, believed to have been brought over to England by Saxon (or Jutish) invaders, and England's mixed government was often referred to as 'our old Gothick Constitution'. Furthermore, the Reformation could be regarded as the North's rescuing of humanity, for the second time, from the decadence and tyranny of the Roman South. 'Gothic' therefore came to imply an amalgam of all these moral and cultural values, and no building could better have summed up the Whig vision or Patriot protest. The Gothic Temple was dedicated specifically 'To the Liberty of our Ancestors'. Round it were placed the seven Saxon Deities, transported from the western side of the gardens; on the ceiling of its dome were painted the arms of Cobham's Saxon forebears; and over the door was placed a fine Gothic inscription from Corneille's play *Horace* (1639), which may be translated thus: 'I thank the Gods that I am not a Roman.' Implied was the second line of the couplet: 'So as to keep some human feelings still.'

Before the Gothic Temple was completed, Walpole fell from power and, once the common enemy had gone, the Patriot alliance crumbled, discrediting sections of the garden programme. Horace Walpole, the Prime Minister's son, who visited Stowe in 1753, protested that he had 'no patience at building and planting a satire',[2] and he was right about the folly of erecting monuments on the shifting sands of a political manifesto. But Cobham's original plan of presenting an ideal political vision through the buildings, statues and inscriptions of a garden was surely a noble concept, and enough still survives of his extraordinary sermon in stone to intrigue, and perhaps challenge, an open-minded visitor.

2

Stowe before
Viscount Cobham

The Temple family of Stowe claimed descent from Leofric and his wife Lady Godiva, thus forming a link with the Saxon earls of Mercia. The earliest documentary evidence, however, locates them as yeoman sheep farmers near Witney in Oxfordshire. By 1546 Peter Temple was renting a sheep farm at Burton Dasset in Warwickshire, and in 1571 he took the lease of Stowe. The manor of Stowe had been confiscated at the Norman Conquest and given by King William to his half-brother, Odo, Bishop of Bayeux. By 1149 it belonged to the abbey of Osney at Oxford and, eight years after the dissolution of the monasteries in 1539, it had become part of the endowment for the new bishopric of Oxford. Peter Temple was probably attracted by the suitability of the estate for sheep, but no less by the fact that the local town of Buckingham, one of the old rotten boroughs, had two MPs elected by only 13 voters.

Peter's son, John, inherited the lease of Stowe in 1578, aged 36, and bought the manor outright 11 years later. He married a kinswoman of the Spencers of Althorp and was appointed a JP and high sheriff of Buckinghamshire. In thus establishing his family at Stowe, he evidently deserved the description of 'frugal and provident'[3].

In contrast John's son Thomas, who inherited Stowe in 1603 aged about 37, was ambitious to the point of overreaching himself. He bought a knighthood on James I's accession in 1603 and then a baronetcy in 1611, as soon as the new order was created. He was a lawyer of Lincoln's Inn and, like his father, served as a JP and sheriff of Oxfordshire (1606), Buckinghamshire (1616) and Warwickshire (1620); he was also an MP in 1588–89. His wife lived to see over 700 blood descendants, but the economic depression of the 1620s and his numerous surviving children led him into debt; his nine daughters needed marriage portions of £1500 each, and his second son, John, cost some £16,000 to establish at Staunton Barry (now part of Milton Keynes). His eldest son, Peter, married Anne Throckmorton and thus

Sir Richard Temple, the third Baronet, in a painting attributed to Henry Gascars; it dates from about 1673–78, when he was building the core of the present Stowe House and was about to lay out his Parlour Garden

[overleaf]
The vista stretching from the centre of the house's south front down to the lake formed the spine of the garden

S.ᴿ R: TEMPLE
1634~1699

acquired the Luffield estate, north of Stowe. Already by 1625
Stowe woods were laid out with ridings, early evidence of Stowe's
development as a designed landscape. Sir Thomas was forced to sell
land, and used the proceeds to add to the Burton Dassett estate, in
contravention of an agreement with Peter. When he was sued for the
money by Peter, he handed Stowe over to his son in 1630 and retired
to live with a daughter in Warwickshire.

Sir Peter – he too had bought a knighthood, in 1609 aged 17 –
established a large park at Stowe. Documents show that a park had
existed in the early thirteenth century, and in 1572 there is reference to
a small 'Old Park'. This was probably the 'Owlde Parke', covering
77 acres and mentioned in Abraham Allen's survey of 1633; it was
doubtless the area known by 1719 as Home Park, where Cobham made
his first garden. Sir Peter's first wife had died in 1619/20, and the year
he took over Stowe he made a second marriage, to Christian Leveson,
who brought with her a dowry of £3000. He soon arranged for Allen's
survey to be made, prior to enclosing the common fields in 1649. By
then most of the villagers seem to have moved from the area around
the parish church of St Mary to the neighbouring hamlets of Dadford
and Lamport. This allowed Sir Peter to enclose a new park of 200 acres
to the north-east of Stowe House, for which he purchased a herd of
deer from Lord Spencer at nearby Wicken in 1651.

Sir Peter gained notoriety for quarrelling with his brother, suing his
father, and being openly rebuked in Parliament for maltreating his
daughter. He was also an MP and high sheriff, facing severe difficulties
when he was required to collect Charles I's hated ship money tax, first
imposed on non-coastal towns in 1634. During the civil war, financial
problems forced him to pawn his plate; when he died in 1653 he was
in debt to 105 creditors for some £26,000.

Sir Richard succeeded as third baronet aged 19 and still a minor.
He was rightly described as 'the fountain of exemplary contrivances'[4]
and, after most of his estates had been legally managed by his creditors
for three years, succeeded in rectifying matters by mortgaging some
of his properties to buy off over £19,000 worth of debts for £7,000.
As MP for Buckingham he cultivated its 13 voters assiduously, most
famously in offering the timber needed to rebuild the town hall in
1679. He was thereafter known as 'Sir Timber Temple'. In 1672,
as part of an ongoing campaign to consolidate and extend his land
holdings, he regained Westbury woods, south-west of Stowe. He was
an MP for almost 40 years, becoming an expert on parliamentary
precedent. In the 1660s he suffered from chronic indigestion. In 1672
he became commissioner of the customs, with a handsome salary of
£2000. Three years later he married Mary Knapp, whose inheritance

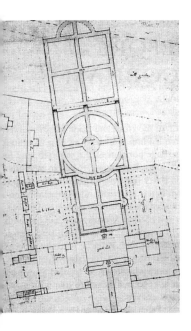

One of the schemes
drafted around 1680,
when Sir Richard Temple
was planning the new
Parlour Garden, south of
his new house, together
with the avenues
stretching down to the
later Octagon Lake

[overleaf]
The south front and Sir
Richard Temple's Parlour
Garden, probably as first
constructed about 1683.
This small formal garden
was replaced by
Bridgeman's parterres in
1717, which were in turn
removed in 1742 to form
the present sweeping
lawn

of £4000 allowed him in 1676 to begin the construction of a new
mansion, still the core of today's house. Designed by William Cleare,
it cost £2600.

Just before this Sir Richard had begun to improve his estate,
planting a vineyard in 1668, and constructing a walled kitchen garden
for apple and pear orchards near the present Menagerie in 1671–73. In
about 1680, as soon as the new house was approaching completion, he
began to plan the new 'Parlour Garden', stretching 200 yards south of
the house, between the old Hey Way to the east and his recently built
walled garden to the west. This replaced the 'oulde garden' west of the
church, but allowed the retention of what were probably outbuildings
from the old house, including the barn, stable, timber yard and hog
houses. The series of 16 proposals now in the Huntington Library,
California, shows various schemes for dealing with a major problem:
reconciling the alignment of the new house, which faced south-east
towards the just-visible steeple (blown down in 1699 and never fully
rebuilt) of Buckingham's original medieval church three miles away,
with the north–south axis of the old house and the associated east–west
Cross Lane. He laid out three levels of parterres or compartments as far
as the Cross Lane. This stretched westward from the church and later
became the Great Cross Walk; previously it had no doubt served as
a cattle route from the old farmhouse to the hog pond and the later
Home Park.

Around 1694, the indefatigable traveller Celia Fiennes described
the gardens as 'one below another with low breast walls and tareas
[terrace] walkes … replenished with all ye Curiosityes or Requisites for
ornament, pleasure and use, beyond it are orchards and woods, with
rows of trees.'[5] The Parlour Garden was planted with rows of cherry
and apple trees in 1682, and by 1683 there were two fountains, one
in a circular basin, as the gardener preferred, rather than oval, as Sir
Richard had wished, and one over seven feet high. It is just possible
that two letters with advice from Sir Christopher Wren refer to the
pipes and gates needed for this garden;[6] William Cleare, Sir Richard's
architect, was also Wren's chief master-joiner.

Two other features completed the new grounds. South of the formal
garden, a narrow avenue of poplars was planted in 1682. This Abele
Walk extended the vista towards the fishponds at the bottom of the
valley, where the Octagon Lake now lies. West of the walled garden,
the wilderness was laid out in 1683. Its semicircular spread of paths lay
south of the site of the later Temple of Bacchus, stretching towards the
line of the Roman road between Bicester and Towcester. For the last
15 years of his life, Sir Richard seems to have enjoyed his new garden
without making significant changes.

The South Prospect

Rich? Temple hou? at Stow=Langport

3

Viscount Cobham

S ir Richard Temple, the fourth baronet, inherited Stowe in 1697,
aged 21. He made his mark nationally as both a general and a Whig
politician. It is as the creator of Stowe's seminal garden that he is now
best known, however, and this was partly the unforeseen fruit of time
spent in the political wilderness. After Eton and Christ's College,
Cambridge, he became MP for Buckingham. He was made colonel
of one of the three new regiments of foot raised in 1702, aged 26, and
then served in Marlborough's European campaigns. By 1710 he had
been appointed lieutenant-general, one of only five British officers of
such a rank serving in Flanders.

During this time Sir Richard was also strengthening the family's
dynastic ties. Two of his sisters, Christian and Hester, were married in
1708 and 1710 to Sir Thomas Lyttelton of Hagley and Richard Grenville
of Wotton respectively. Both matches proved important in the history of
Stowe, not least because their descendants were included in the special
remainder attached to Sir Richard's viscountcy in 1718, providing for
heirs should he die childless. In contrast, the line of his eldest sister
Maria was excluded because she had married the Rev. Richard West,
merely his regimental chaplain, against his wishes. In 1717 he bought out
for £7000 his second cousins William and Peter Temple, who would
otherwise have inherited Stowe if he had died childless.

His financial position improved rapidly. In addition to his army
income and various sinecures, such as constable of Windsor Castle from
1716, his marriage the previous year to Anne Halsey, a brewery heiress,
brought in £20,000, while his lucrative involvement in the brief British
occupation of the Spanish port of Vigo in 1719 enabled him to
undertake further extensive work on his house and garden. His social
standing had also significantly risen. Although he was dismissed from
the army by the Tories in October 1713, when Jonathan Swift called
him 'the greatest Whig in the army',[7] he was rewarded at the accession
of King George I the following year by being raised to the peerage. He

[above]
**Bust of Lord Cobham
in Roman dress, by Peter
Scheemakers**

[right]
**A statue of Lord Cobham,
dressed as a Roman
general, surmounts the
Cobham Monument,
which is his garden
memorial**

The Queen's Theatre, seen from the Rotondo, *c.*1733–34, by Jacques Rigaud

took the title of Baron Cobham from his grandmother's line, emphasising his own allegiance to the new Hanoverian monarchs by recalling an earlier Lord Cobham's opposition to the accession of the first Stuart king of England, James I. Four years later he was created Viscount Cobham and granted the special remainder. Thus by 1719, aged 44, he had acquired the means and standing to make Stowe match his ambitions, having by then faced and resolved so many challenges; as his contemporary James Craggs noted, he was a man 'who does not hate a difficulty',[8] a theme echoed by Pope with regard to Cobham's gardening in his verse *Epistle to Lord Burlington* (1731) in praise of the new informal style.

In the first decade after he inherited Stowe, Sir Richard was too busy to make much change on the estate. It was not until 1711 that he turned his attention to the garden and house. In October that year, Lady Fermanagh recorded that 'he makes great improvements in ye gardens'.[9] He began by reshaping his father's Parlour Garden south of the house, opening out the three small terraces into a vast formal parterre with a large basin and fountain, and in 1717 adding the Sundial Parlour nearby.

In 1713–14 the garden staff averaged only six men, but by 1718–19 his rapidly growing wealth allowed Lord Cobham to increase numbers to nearly 30. Thereafter he contracted out many of the tasks, under foremen such as John Gurnit, John Lee, William Nelson, Thomas Pease, Frank Rogers and William Turpin, some of whom are still recalled in the names of the walks they built. The massive operations are evident from bills like the blacksmith's, for the ironwork of 30 new wheelbarrows between October 1715 and the following March. Nothing could hinder the progress, even when Edward Bissell, the head gardener from 1716, had to be carried around on a specially adapted chair after he broke his leg in October 1718. In July 1719, Vanbrugh wrote to Jacob Tonson that Lord Cobham was already spending 'all he has to spare'

Portrait of Mr Bridgeman,
by William Hogarth,
1725–30, oil on canvas

on improving his house and garden, something with which he was 'much entertain'd'.[10]

After the south side, Lord Cobham turned to the northern approach. The Course was planted with avenues of elms in 1712, a canal was dug in 1716–18, and a mount was constructed in 1716–17 where the two met. In 1718–19 he developed the triangle west of the house, towards Lee's Bastion on Nelson's Walk, beginning in 1718 with the two-storey heated greenhouse or Orangery and the first garden buildings, such as the Temple of Bacchus and Nelson's Seat (both now gone). In 1719–20 he made his first hesitant moves into Home Park, refilling an early ha-ha when he decided to extend the garden even further. The Rotondo and the Queen's Theatre (now gone) came next, allowing the garden to spread to the Octagon Lake and the Lake Pavilions by 1722–23. This valley and lake provided a new and dramatic entrance for visitors at the bottom of the garden, a plan which must have been in place from 1717, when the New Inn on the old Buckingham road was built.

Lord Cobham's direct involvement in laying out the garden is always apparent: in 1714 he told his steward that he would 'be down in ten days and will then give directions about the step'.[11] Nevertheless, to help realise his gardening ambitions, Lord Cobham called on Charles Bridgeman, later the royal gardener but here at the beginning of his career, and his Kit-Cat friend, the architect Sir John Vanbrugh, who designed the Rotondo and, probably, the Lake Pavilions for him. The earliest record of Bridgeman's involvement is a bill for £1 2s 6d paid to 'Mr Bridgeman's man', probably from 1714. Later that decade a letter states that 'My Lord wood not have it donn till Mr Bridgman Coms'.[12]

Bridgeman's bird's-eye view of the new garden, *c.*1719, emphasises the key position of the Rotondo

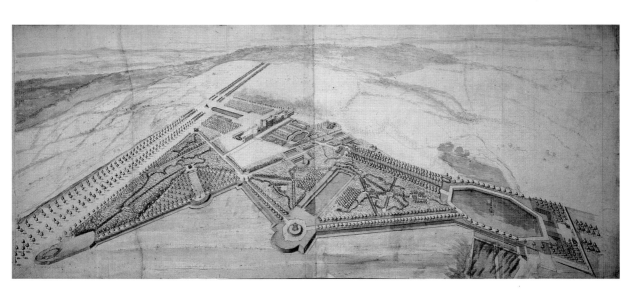

By 1724 Lord Perceval noted that 'Bridgeman laid out the ground and plan'd the whole, which cannot fail of recommending him to business.'[13] The garden by now comprised 28 acres and more than ten buildings, leading Lord Perceval to add that Stowe had already gained 'the reputation of being the finest seat in England'.[14] He was particularly impressed by the use Bridgeman made of the ha-ha, allowing continuous vistas into the surrounding countryside without the unsightly and unnatural intervention of fences or walls. Its first recorded appearance at Stowe was as a 'stockade ditch' south of Lime Walk in February 1719, and it was used frequently thereafter by Bridgeman.

Vanbrugh's first recorded visit was in June 1719, but he may have helped Lord Cobham earlier, after being banished from Blenheim in 1716, following arguments with the Duchess of Marlborough. His first garden buildings at Stowe, the 'little house' and 'sumer hous' (possibly Nelson's Seat and the Temple of Bacchus, but now gone), date from 1719, the Rotondo from 1720–21, and he also did much to enlarge the house. Vanbrugh obviously loved Stowe; in 1725 he spent two weeks there with his wife and Lord Carlisle of Castle Howard, telling Tonson that Stowe was 'a Place now, so Agreeable, that I had much ado to leave it at all'.[15] In March 1726 Vanbrugh died, and so Lord Cobham brought in another leading architect, James Gibbs, despite the latter's Tory tendencies. That September, Gibbs and Bridgeman were together at Stowe, and in May 1727 Gibbs was given 20 guineas. About 60 acres were added to the garden to the south-west and Home Park was enclosed by a ha-ha, providing a rural pastoral setting within the garden's terrace walks. The bottom of the valley was dammed to create the Eleven-Acre Lake. During his first period of employment in the 1720s, Gibbs added the two Boycott Pavilions on the brow of a hill on

[above left]
Sir John Vanbrugh, painted by Sir Godfrey Kneller for the Kit-Cat Club, of which Vanbrugh, Cobham and Kneller were all members

[above right]
James Gibbs, who designed most of the garden temples in the Hawkwell Field, by John Michael Williams, c.1752

the road from Oxford, marking the entrance to the gardens from the park, and the Temple of Fame, known as Gibbs's Building, and later moved north to become the Fane of Pastoral Poetry. Around 1730 Gibbs was supplanted by William Kent, one of the pioneers of the eighteenth-century landscape garden. Kent's Temple of Venus dates from 1731 and was his first major contribution to the landscape at Stowe. Facing north across the Eleven-Acre Lake, it effectively completed the western garden.

Lord Cobham was famous not only for his military, political and gardening exploits, but also for his wide range of friends. He moved in a circle of wits and poets which included poet and dramatist William Congreve, a Kit-Cat Club friend like Vanbrugh. In 1728 Congreve praised Lord Cobham by addressing him in one of his poems:

Graceful in Form, and winning in Address
While well you think, what aptly you express,
With Health, with Honour, with a fair Estate,
A Table free, and elegantly neat.
What can be added more to mortal Bliss?
What can he want who stands possest of this?[16]

Even better known as a poet was Alexander Pope, who is recorded as a frequent visitor to Stowe from September 1724. The following year he noted that he was 'still returning to Lord Cobham's [garden] with fresh satisfaction',[17] visiting it and Wotton, and going again the next year with Jonathan Swift and John Gay. In 1731 he wrote the *Epistle to Lord Burlington*, his famous poem promoting the new more informal style of gardening, choosing as his prime example Lord Cobham's work at Stowe. In a letter the same year he confided: 'If any thing under Paradise could set me beyond all Earthly Cogitations; Stowe might do it. It is much more beautiful than when I saw it before.'[18] Following the death of his mother, it was to Stowe that Pope chose to retire. James Hammond, a minor poet who died at Stowe ten years later, wrote in 1732:

To Stowe's delightful scenes I now repair,
In Cobham's smile to lose the gloom of care.[19]

Similarly in 1738 another poet, Paul Whitehead, again praised Lord Cobham's virtue and friendliness:

Ask ye, What's Honour? I'll the truth impart,
Know, honour then, is Honesty of Heart.
To the sweet scenes of social Stow repair,
And search the Master's breast – You'll find it there.[20]

Such frequent comments on Lord Cobham's affability conflict with tales about his harsh nature. Notably severe in his dealings with lawbreakers, the tradition that he had the Silverstone poachers killed in 1736 is probably a local exaggeration of their awful but less final punishment

Gibbs' Boycott Pavilions marked the entrance to the park from the Oxford road

of transportation in 1736, but in 1741 his reprimand to his steward, William Roberts, 'a great favourite of Lord Cobham, ... vex'd him so much that he made away with himself.'[21] The milder side of Lord Cobham's character is seen in 1734, when Mr Berkeley recorded how 'two coachfuls of us' visiting from Rousham had intended only to dine at Stowe, but had actually stayed three days, since 'it is enchanted ground, and not in people's power to leave when they please. Stowe is in great beauty, the master of it in good health and excellent spirits.'[22] Indeed, on this occasion 'Pope diverted us by translating Horace'. Lord Cobham's generosity is evident in his rebuilding of part of Buckingham after the fire of 1725.

To allow the garden's extension eastwards, Lord Cobham rerouted the approach from Buckingham to the western side of the house in about 1732. This coincided with his retirement from politics for the second time in 1733 to take up residence at Stowe, following the loss of his regiment because of his opposition to Walpole's excise scheme. Thus many of the temples which he added in this part of the garden reflect in their iconography Cobham's dislike of Walpole and his love of freedom from corruption and tyranny. He enclosed 40 acres in the small but exquisite valley now known as the Elysian Fields, in which

The Temple of Ancient Virtue in the Elysian Fields

Kent constructed two of his best buildings, the Temple of British
Worthies and the Temple of Ancient Virtue. Kent's Shell Bridge
formed a link between the two temples across the old millstream, now
dammed to form the Alder and Worthies rivers, and echoed the Grotto
which he placed at the north end of the waterway. These are set in one
of his earliest and most charming examples of naturalistic landscaping.
In 1739 Pope wrote to Martha Blount: 'I never saw this Place in half the
beauty & perfection it now has. … This Garden is beyond description
[in] the New part of it, I am every hour in it, but dinner & night, and
every hour Envying myself the delight of it.'[23] As Joseph Spence later
commented, 'Lord Cobham began in the Bridgeman taste. 'tis the
Elysian Fields that is the painting part of his gardens.'[24]

Although he reached the age of 60 in 1735, Lord Cobham remained
fully abreast of changes in gardening taste, if not leading them himself.
Lord Perceval in 1724 had noted 'my Lords good taste' in regard to
Bridgeman's semi-formal plan, where 'nothing is more irregular in the
whole, nothing more regular in the parts'.[25] Kent's new naturalistic
approach of the 1730s heightened the tension between formalising 'art'
and liberating 'nature', a contrast which must have appealed to Lord
Cobham's enthusiasm for political liberty. James Thomson's long
patriotic poem *Liberty* (1736) included the lines:

See: Sylvan scenes, where art alone pretends
To dress her mistress and disclose her charms –
Such as a Pope in miniature has shown,
… And such as form a Richmond, Chiswick, Stowe.

In 1742, Samuel Boyse called his poem describing Stowe *The Triumphs
of Nature* and began it by addressing 'Delightful Nature', admitting that:

Here Art attends – and waits thy ruling will,
For she at best is but thy hand-maid still.

It was in fact in 1742 that Cobham began to obliterate and naturalise
the grand parterre which he himself had installed only 25 years before.
Nevertheless, others thought of Stowe as still primarily a formal garden
dominated by classical buildings. Joseph Warton, in his ode *The
Enthusiast* or *The Lover of Nature* (1744), wrote: 'Can Stow with all her

attic fanes, such raptures raise As the thrush haunted copse?' In 1738
Bishop Herring admitted that at Stowe he would have 'beheld with
contempt an artificial ruin',[26] around the very time that Lord Cobham
constructed the Artificial Ruins near the Octagon Cascade. Similarly,
the Marchioness Grey complained of Stowe that 'Nature has done very
little for it, & Art so much that you cannot possibly be deceived.'[27]
Yet Stowe's natural charms could still please. Elizabeth Montague
in 1744 wrote how 'Stowe … is beyond description, it gives the best
idea of Paradise that can be'.[28]

The Artificial Ruins were
a relatively late addition
to the gardens by
Cobham

The 1730s must have seen the height of Lord Cobham's entertaining
at Stowe, especially once it had become his opposition power base after
1733. Here he trained his 'mob' of nephews, part of the 'Patriot band'
who eventually brought about Walpole's downfall in 1742. Since 1727,
when his brother-in-law Richard Grenville had died, the latter's son
Richard and his four brothers and one sister, all aged 16 or under, had
been all but adopted by Lord Cobham. There were 13 nephews in all,
including Gilbert West, whose poem *Stowe* (1732) provided one of the
earliest detailed descriptions of the garden. Another nephew, George
Lyttelton, and the younger Richard Grenville, later Earl Temple, both
visited the classical sites of Italy. They then returned to support their
uncle as MPs, and spent much time with him at Stowe during the
1730s; indeed many of the inscriptions on statues and buildings were
composed or selected by Lyttelton. The Temple of Friendship, with
its set of ten marble busts, recalled the political alliances of 1739, and
especially the visit two years earlier of the Prince of Wales, along with
Lords Chesterfield and Westmorland, all honoured with busts. Other
visitors included Whig politician William Pulteney, Lady Suffolk
(Lyttelton composed an epigram for the bust planned for her at Stowe),
Pope's friend Martha Blount, Hammond and, of course, Pope, who
in 1739 described a typical day: 'Everyone takes a different way, and
wanders about till we meet at noon. At mornings we breakfast and
dispute; after dinner, and at night, music and harmony; in the garden
fishing; no politics and no cards, nor much reading.'[29]

The most famous of the 'Boy Patriots', however, only became
a nephew by marriage, and that after Lord Cobham's death. This was
the future prime minister William Pitt, the contemporary at Eton of
Richard Grenville and George Lyttelton. Lady Irwin described him as
'a very pretty speaker, one the Prince [of Wales] is partial to, and under
the tuition of Lord Cobham'.[30] Like Lord Cobham, he was deprived by
Walpole of his army place and like the rest of the 'mob' he spent much
time at Stowe. The love-sick Hammond wrote in 1732:

There [at Stowe] Pit, in manner soft, in friendship warm,
With mild advice my listening grief shall charm.

In 1735 Pitt entered Parliament for Old Sarum, the rottenest of boroughs, but he spent the four months from July to October at Stowe. Here he amused himself with various games, noting: 'I was very stupid and play'd very well at cricket.'[31] Another visitor and possible player was Lady Suffolk, who explained how 'I have learnt all the theory of cricket, and have some thoughts of practising this afternoon', despite her age of 47.[32] No doubt she was an easy prey to the charm of flattery, since she recalled how 'Lord Cobham says I am the best-looking woman of *thirty* that he ever saw'.[33] Pitt became so closely associated with Stowe that James Thomson, who spent much of 1734 and 1735 there, imagines in his poem *Autumn* (1744) enjoying his conversation above all others' at Stowe:

And there, O Pitt! thy country's early boast,
There let me sit beneath the sheltered slopes,
Or in that Temple where, in future times,
Thou well shall merit a distinguished name,
And, with thy converse blest, catch the last smiles
Of Autumn beaming o'er the yellow woods.

[below]
The Temple of Friendship celebrated the political alliances which were Cobham's inspiration for his garden

[overleaf]
The Palladian Bridge

Not surprisingly, as Lord Cobham's cubs became more effective
at worrying Walpole, so Lord Cobham's confidence in building
a political satire also grew. The allegorical meaning of the painting
on the Temple of Friendship's ceiling (see page 13) was not difficult to
understand, while the nearby Imperial Closet (another building by
Gibbs, long since gone, which celebrated the benign rule of the Roman
Flavian emperors), the statue of *The Fighting Gladiator* and the Palladian
Bridge, with its references to Whig trade policy (see page 14), all helped
express Cobham's opposition to Walpole and his supporters. The
startlingly original Gothic Temple or Temple of Liberty, designed by
James Gibbs in a second briefer burst of activity at Stowe in 1739–42,
to crown Hawkwell Field in the newly developed eastern part of the
garden, was the culmination of his iconographical building.

Lord Cobham's sense of humour is apparent in his choice of
a damaged and headless statue for the ruined Temple of Modern
Virtue, sited next, and in careful contrast, to the resplendent Temple
of Ancient Virtue. He was never very sympathetic to the established
church, giving more prominence to a Witch's House (now gone) and
to Temples of Venus and Bacchus than to the old parish church of
St Mary, which was concealed by planting. Although he employed
able architects, his style was eclectic, mixing Saxon with Greek, Roman
and Chinese motifs for primarily political purposes; the Shell Rotondo,
supposedly his only design and now gone, was equally individualistic.

In 1741 Lord Cobham was looking for a new gardener to succeed
William Love. He wanted someone 'able to converse instructively on
his favourite pursuit, but free from the vanity and conceit which had
made his former assistants disinclined to alterations upon which he had
determined.'[34] His choice was Lancelot Brown, then aged 25 and at
an early stage in his career, before he became known as 'Capability'
Brown. With Brown's help the last major new area, another 60 acres,
was added to the garden on its north-eastern corner, forming the
Grecian Valley. Slight hints of disagreement still persisted. Gibbs's
published plan for the Queen's Temple was changed before it was
used, and the channelled flutes which Brown added to the Cobham
Monument dominating the valley were 'not authorised by Gibbs',
according to Earl Temple in 1765. The Grecian Temple begun in 1747,
by far the largest and grandest of Stowe's temples and now known as
the Temple of Concord and Victory, was significantly modified only
five years later. Even the area linking these buildings, the magnificent
Grecian Valley itself, caused further problems. Although eager to finish
'the head of the oval', Brown assured Lord Cobham in 1746: 'I had
never formed any other idea on it than what your Lordship gave me.'[35]
Indeed, visitors in 1748 reported several unexecuted plans for the floor
of the valley, while in 1746 Anne Grenville referred to Stowe as 'the

Lancelot 'Capability'
Brown, who was head
gardener at Stowe
1741–51 and designed
the Grecian Temple, by
Nathaniel Dance (detail)

house of Discord'.[36] It is just possible that Richard Grenville's radical views on the need to naturalise the garden were partly responsible. The Chinese House, which was originally erected in the Elysian Fields (and from its mention in an anonymous 1738 description of Stowe may claim to be the earliest garden building in England designed in this style), was transferred to Grenville's garden at Wotton in late 1748, when Lord Cobham removed it from this inappropriate site, and it stayed there for over 200 years. Grenville had also countermanded his uncle's instructions to remove the plate from Stowe during the rebellion of 1745, and three years later he was responsible for building the Old Gaol in Buckingham after proposing a bill which Stanhope described as 'the arrantest job that was ever brought to Parliament'.[37] Nevertheless, we have a picture of relative harmony in Cobham's last years from his

The Grecian Valley, designed by Brown, was the last major new area in Cobham's garden

[left]
The Cobham Monument

niece Hester, who recorded in 1748 that 'riding or walking is the amusement of the morning & Homer and cards of the evening'.[38] A month later she reported that 'my Lord tells us every night it does not signifie to read unless we know how we apply what we read',[39] and there was talk of a play to be enacted a few months later.

By the time of his death in 1749, Lord Cobham had established the present garden's framework and started its naturalisation. He had landscaped 205 acres, built over three dozen temples, laid out eight lakes or ponds, planted numerous avenues, built some four miles of ha-ha, had over 50 inscriptions carved, purchased over 40 busts and nearly 50 statues for the garden, and had the interiors of 12 garden buildings decorated with wall and ceiling paintings. His garden monument is the pillar supposedly erected to his honour by his wife in 1747–49, from which he could view his great achievement. The column is 104 feet high, and on top his statue (replaced in 2001 after the original was destroyed by lightning) stands, at 3.14 m (10ft 4in), much larger than life-size and suitably Roman in dress. Like Lucullus, he had proved himself a great general, grandee, gourmet and gardener.

[below]
The Chinese House, originally erected in the Elysian Fields but soon removed from Stowe

4

Earl Temple

Richard Grenville, later Earl Temple, succeeded his uncle at Stowe in 1749. He had long been groomed for the task and had developed his own ideas about gardening and architecture. Until 1770, however, he took an active part in politics, initially in conjunction with his brother, George Grenville, and his brother-in-law, William Pitt, Earl of Chatham, both of whom served as prime minister (1763–65 and 1766–68 respectively). In 1760 he became a knight of the Garter, although he never achieved his proud ambition of a dukedom. In 1761 he resigned as lord privy seal and four years later he refused to become first lord of the treasury under his brother-in-law, instead using all his resources to attack Pitt's government. The death of his brother George in 1770 prompted his final withdrawal from public life.

In 1737 Grenville had married Anna Chamber, an heiress from Middlesex with £50,000, at Lady Suffolk's Marble Hill House in Twickenham. Their only child died young and therefore Grenville too was succeeded by his nephew, George's son, another George. On his mother's death in 1752, Richard Grenville was described by his cousin Sir George Lyttelton as the richest subject in England. Much of this wealth he used to refine the garden and, from 1770, to give the house its present magnificent fronts.

From the first, Richard Grenville was eager to alter the garden. In 1750 he brought in a new gardener, Richard Woodward, from his old family home at Wotton, although he did not technically inherit Stowe until two years later, and he parted amicably with 'Capability' Brown in autumn 1751. He certainly had no qualms about making significant changes, since that very year he enraged his uncle's widow, now retired to Stoke Poges, by introducing sheep into the garden. Although this pastoral element could be seen as the logical extension of an idealised Arcadian scene, Lady Cobham complained to Brown, whom she was employing at Stoke, that 'if my Lord Cobham cou'd know how Stow was used how vext he would be'.[40] Grenville's sister

Allan Ramsay's imposing portrait has captured well Earl Temple's sense of his own importance

Temple's first priority was to naturalise the landscape he had inherited, giving the lakes a softer, more natural margin

Hester, married to William Pitt, was also said to be 'in an uproar' over the sheep, and later lamented the alterations to the form and shapes of her husband's 'dear paths' in the walks: 'Upon the whole their Beauty is Greater but their Merit less.'[41]

Temple's main emphasis at first was to naturalise the remaining formal areas of his uncle's garden, and from 1751 to 1753 he was principally concerned to soften the landscape. This was done by filling in the inward-facing ha-has of the Home Park and Hawkwell Field, removing the straight edges from the Octagon and Eleven-Acre Lakes, filling in the small formal canals on the North Lawn and east of the Rotondo, and reducing unnecessary avenues to clumps of specimen trees by felling along Gurnet's Walk and most of the Great Cross Walk.

The speed with which Temple effected these naturalising changes is evident from Pococke's comment in May 1751: 'This place, now the trees are grown up appears much finer than it did formerly, and some alterations have been made by the present Lord in great taste.'[42] In July Elizabeth Grenville, his sister-in-law, wrote that she liked 'most of the alterations extremely particularly the Queen Theatre & the Gothick feild'[43] – the Queen's Theatre had lost its shepherds and shepherdesses. It also seems that Temple was ambitious to publicise the garden more widely, encouraging or allowing a free market in guidebooks. He could not conceal his pride in his achievements at Stowe, asserting in his poem *Stowe or the Hill of Hills* that they surpassed the best that nature could offer in Greece and Italy:

Tell me no more of Tempe's vale,
Nor boast of Arno's flowery dale,
Taste must confess, superior still,
The charms which decorate my Hill.

After the landscape had been largely naturalised, Earl Temple was able to turn his attention to classicising the garden buildings. Although he may have started by altering the Artificial Ruins in 1751–58, the architect responsible for most of the changes during the 1750s was Giovanni Battista Borra. He was employed, from 1752, on modifying the Grecian Temple (now the Temple of Concord and Victory), perhaps because of his knowledge of the similar Graeco-Roman temple at Baalbec, which he had visited the year before. Borra went on to modify the Rotondo in 1752–54, Gibbs's Building (now the Fane of Pastoral Poetry) in 1756, and the Boycott Pavilions in 1758–60. Earl Temple also had several smaller structures moved, including Coucher's Obelisk (now gone) in about 1751, the Guglio (an obelisk which stood in the centre of the Octagon Lake and can be seen in Rigaud's engraving) in 1754, and in 1756 the Grenville Column, commemorating the death in naval battle of Temple's brother Captain Thomas Grenville in 1747, along with many statues.

By the mid-1750s, having restructured most of the landscape and a significant number of its buildings, Temple naturally turned to the problem of rebuilding the house. The south front was by this time an unattractive muddle of his uncle's ever larger additions. By 1753 Borra had supplied an impressive scheme for rebuilding, one that featured in many publications for several decades as actually constructed. In 1755, however, it seems that William Pitt pointed out some crucial difficulties in Borra's plan and Earl Temple applauded him: 'Where the Devil you picked up all this architectural skill, what Palladio you have studied

The Temple of Concord and Victory, originally designed by Capability Brown, shown here in 1796-97 by artist Thomas Medland

I know not, but you are an Architect born & I am edifyed & delighted.'[44] He added, about his brother James: 'So is Jemmy, that Goth, that visigoth, that antipodes of taste; He enters now fully into all the glorys of our future front.'[45] In fact all that came of this initial attempt at the south front was the double flight of steps designed jointly by Borra and Earl Temple in the Servants' Hall in 1754.

It was perhaps not surprising that his concern for the house and other matters let his enthusiasm for the garden wane for a time. In October 1756, however, Elizabeth Grenville told Pitt: 'Lord Temple has once again caught the flame of gardening & says it now burns as bright as ever at which I think all his friends much rejoice from the great pleasure it affords him.'[46] The extent of the further changes is evident from Hester Pitt's regrets as expressed to her husband: 'I cannot now follow your dear Paths in any of the Walks. Their Form and Shape is totally Alter'd.'[47] The only exceptions left unchanged were some of the earliest naturalised elements, such as the parterre. John Adam, brother of the more famous Robert, observed similarly in 1759: 'The formality and stiffness that formally prevailed in one quarter is now converted into more natural and easy forms. Most of the hedges are taken away and the trees thinned in such a manner as to have a beautiful effect on the scenery.'[48] He complained of a defect, a swelling which has 'but one half in the garden and the other half left out', but admits that it is more likely to be an oversight than 'a scrimpedness or doing things by Halves', since the size of the garden and the number of buildings 'show forth a princely disregard for money'.[49]

Earl Temple was soon back to his proud form, telling Hester in 1761: 'I am extravagantly in love – with Stowe; Sacharissa and amoret united! never, never was any thing half so fine and charming.'[50] At about this time, after radically altering the garden inside the ha-ha, he turned his attention to the wider landscape outside, especially the three approach drives, increasing their grandeur by abandoning naturalistic landscaping for the impressive formality of straight roads and avenues. In 1760 he built the Oxford Bridge and formed the Oxford Water, moving Kent's gate-piers to their present position. Further out he added a pair of Ionic lodges at Water Stratford, presumably laying out the straight road in between. In the same year he built another pair of Ionic lodges at Luffield, to mark the northern end of the Silverstone drive. All this must have meant sweeping away hedges and fences to improve the drives and enlarge the park, which by 1775 had grown to 585 acres. Finally, in about 1775, following the enclosure of Radclive-cum-Chackmore, he laid out the Grand or Stowe Avenue to the Corinthian Arch, perhaps his most impressive piece of landscaping. In 1761 Hester reported to William what her brother had lately been doing, 'converting the Quality of the Ground, destroying Hedges, and

making rivers &c.'[51] From 1765 the drive through Culley's Park, linking the Corinthian Arch with the Oxford entrance, enjoyed the magnificent reflection of the east Boycott Pavilion created by the Lower Oxford Water.

Inspired by these improvements, Temple was able to return to altering and moving yet more of the garden buildings. A sudden burst of work in the first half of the 1760s included the demolition of the Sleeping Parlour or Temple of Sleep, probably designed by Vanbrugh; further alterations to the Temple of Concord and Victory; rebuilding the back of the Palladian Bridge and the Temple of Contemplation (the latter now gone); moving Queen Caroline's statue from its original position by the Queen's Theatre to its present position near the western end of the Eleven-Acre Lake; moving Gibbs's Building to become the Fane of Pastoral Poetry; and moving the two Lake Pavilions. With the pressure of an impending royal visit by Princess Amelia in July 1764, he wrote to Hester in late June: 'Love & what is more, Money, will not procure me Masons to reedify fast enough my altered Fabricks. Why cant we move Buildings with as much ease as we do Pictures.'[52] By now little in the garden remained as his uncle had left it, as his cousin George Lyttelton observed the following year: 'The present Master of Stowe has taken off all the Stiffness of the Old Bridgeman Taste, and pulled down some of the Buildings, and altered others that were ugly very much the better; so the Place upon the Whole is vastly improved.'[53]

He did not stop in 1764, however. The key to the next series of improvements was his decision in 1762 to fell the Abele Walk, the poplar avenue stretching from the former parterre down to the Octagon Lake; he called this 'the finest alteration I ever made'.[54] This led in turn to moving the Lake Pavilions further apart in 1764 and building the Corinthian Arch on the horizon in 1765, to the designs of another Pitt, Earl Temple's cousin Thomas, then aged 28. The widened south vista also forced him to implement plans for rebuilding the south front of Stowe House, now exposed from afar. But masterminding the details of numerous alterations was what appealed most to Temple, as he told Hester in January 1769: 'We have passed our time here in the most perfect Solitude, & I can as truly say in the most perfect Content; all the Day with wheelbarrows, all the Evening with Accounts.'[55] He worked hard and reported in 1762: 'I rise every morning a little after five and stick to business very handsomely. I dread the thought of confusion.'[56]

Despite all his changes, Earl Temple made only a few new additions to the garden, two of them in 1778, the year before his death. These were a bridge, symbolically of wood (rebuilt in 2011), and the small Cook Monument, designed on the imperial theme already celebrated

[above]
Temple extended the park as far as the Corinthian Arch

[right]
The statue of Queen Caroline, moved by Temple to its present position

by the Wolfe Obelisk and the Temple of Concord and Victory, to
commemorate Captain James Cook's discoveries in the South Pacific.
His plans for monuments to his brother-in-law William Pitt and his
brother George Grenville were not executed. Cosmetic changes between
1772 and 1775 included work on the Queen's Temple, Nelson's Seat,
Dido's Cave and the Rotondo.

Although he possessed vast wealth, Earl Temple was economical
where possible. In 1750 he transferred the Great Barn from Wotton to
Stowe, and he moved, rather than demolishing, ten different buildings
at Stowe. Some parts, such as elements from the Sleeping Parlour, were
reused, while the balusters from the south front steps went to the
Queen's Temple. Displaced statues from Lord Cobham's vast collection
were redeployed around the Grecian Valley or on the Artificial Ruins.

His crude and brash sense of humour was not well received by
many. It included spitting into Lord Hervey's hat during a reception at
Stowe in 1750 – the outcome of a guinea's bet which he tried to pass off
as a joke. His use of iconography was similarly idiosyncratic. He
commemorated his political protégé, the radical John Wilkes, by giving
the statue of Liberty on the south front of the house a squint like
Wilkes's. Not surprisingly, his political scheming led him to be
considered as the author of the polemical *Letters of Junius*. Horace
Walpole, although happy to accept his hospitality at Stowe, called him
'this malignant man' who 'worked in the mines of successive factions for
over thirty years together'.[57] However, Temple's letters to his sister

[above]
**The south front, with its
commanding vista**

[below]
**The Fane of Pastoral
Poetry**

Hester, where he comes closest to opening his heart, show a more attractive side to his character.[58]

Undisputed were his great pride and ambition, quite oblivious to others' sensibilities. Only 15 days after his uncle Lord Cobham died, he demanded that his mother, Cobham's heiress, should be made a countess so that he could inherit her title. He then demanded the Garter, only acquiring it in 1760 with Pitt's help; George III was so angry that he supposedly threw him the ribbon with his head averted, as a bone is thrown to a dog. Unabashed, Earl Temple then immediately had his new honour featured in the house and on the entrance gateway for all to admire. He was certainly alone in regarding himself as Pitt's political equal; no doubt he intended the Temple of Concord and Victory to be as much a celebration of their political union as of Pitt's victories in the Seven Years' War. Ironically, his obstinate pride led to a serious rift with Pitt from 1765 to 1769, despite Hester's efforts to reconcile the two. Even the intended cenotaph to William Pitt at Stowe was probably to include his own statue. He hoped for a dukedom, but in this he was disappointed.

Earl Temple continued his uncle's custom of using the garden to entertain his numerous visitors. Just as the Grotto had been illuminated during the summer of 1744, soon after its construction, so now it began to form a regular venue for candle-lit suppers with accompanying music. Princess Amelia, King George III's aunt, twice experienced such outdoor amusements during the climatic vagaries

of an English summer. At 10.30pm on Friday 17 July 1764, near the
end of her five days' stay at Stowe, Her Royal Highness walked down
to the Grotto using the new flight of steps on the south front, which
Earl Temple and Horace Walpole found so difficult because of their
gout. The garden was illuminated with 1000 lights and filled with over
1000 spectators. In front of the Grotto an illuminated ship provided
a picturesque platform for the musicians and the Alder river was
covered with floating lights; 20 gallons of oil were burnt in two hours.
'Nothing was seen but lights and people. Nothing was felt but joy and
happiness,' ran one optimistic report.[59] After her cold supper, the
Princess returned before midnight; since it had been raining for the
previous three days, it must have been a cold and damp affair. Lord
Coventry remarked that 'the Stowe party ended badly, the weather
bad, – the wine bad – and the ceremony intolerable.'[60]

On Thursday 5 July 1770, Princess Amelia again braved supper
in the Grotto. This time the cold was so intense that Horace Walpole,
'having some apprehension of the consequence, desired when we came
back a glass of Cherry Brandy by way of prevention.'[61] At least it was
not raining, since after dinner and before the supper that evening they
took coffee at the Doric Arch, initially named Princess Amelia's Arch,
which had been erected by Temple in 1768 in anticipation of the visit,
to provide a suitable entrance to the Elysian Fields and frame the view
to the Palladian Bridge. Horace Walpole had carefully arranged that
a piece of paper with his poem to the Princess should be discovered
in the hand of Apollo's statue nearby. The next day the Princess
was taken fishing on the Eleven-Acre Lake, although some were
embarrassed that she did not succeed in achieving the highest catch.

The Grotto, one of Kent's
creations in the Elysian
Fields, where Earl Temple
entertained royal guests

Other visitors followed their own interests. The Gothick architect
Sanderson Miller, who was at Stowe eight times in
1750, once staying for a whole week, walked in the
garden with the company and Capability Brown for
five hours in November 1749. One morning, perhaps
in 1756, he spent indoors 'with Mr Pitt and Lord
Temple, contriving a finishing to Gibbs building
[the Gothic Temple]', and had 'conversation …
with Mr Pitt and Lord Poulteney etc about
happiness', spending the evening 'singing at the
Grecian Temple'.[62]

The death in 1770 of his brother George
Grenville, the former prime minister, led to Earl
Temple's last and greatest sequence of work at
Stowe, the rebuilding of both grand fronts of the
house. Earl Temple's heir was George's eldest son,
also George, now in his guardianship, and in 1770,

The Doric Arch, initially known as Princess Amelia's Arch in anticipation of the royal visit

to fund the rebuilding of the south front, George offered Earl Temple the considerable income which his father had obtained for him from a government sinecure in 1764 (when he was only 12 years old). The offer spurred Temple into renewed action, although it was several more years before Thomas Pitt's alterations to Robert Adam's plans produced the magnificent façade that we see today, said by Lord Nuneham to surpass 'in majesty and beauty everything I have seen'.[63]

Earl Temple was fully in command throughout. He rejected the advice he had sought from William and Thomas Pitt about the location of gateways on the north front screen walls, and the projecting portico on the south front was said to be his own idea. He was equally ready to criticise Robert Adam's imprecise use of classical details. Not surprisingly, 'the Plans for the Garden Front', as he told Hester in 1770, 'at present ingross most of our Time & Conversation.'[64] He even had the foundations for the south front taken up the next year, apparently to allow for the projection of the south portico. That Temple should have chosen Pitt's graceful simplification of Adam's fussy and unclassical details is a tribute to his now refined taste and judgement.

The effort took its toll, however. In 1772 he confessed to 'many and many disappointments',[65] and the next year Hester wrote that he was 'in no Spirits, and having a bad opinion of Himself'.[66] Two years later he told her: 'I have more than once agreed, when vexed in spirit, with wise King Solomon, that all is Vanity and Vexation.'[67] The following year his wife wanted to abandon Stowe for Eastbury in Dorset, another of their houses, but her husband preferred to soldier on amid the building works. Indeed, despite his serious illness early in 1775, he was still 'wheeled among his workmen', but he had to talk to his steward out of his nurse's sight. Although 'every symptom marked approaching death', he was supposedly saved by 'quantities of wine, & the strongest cordials'.[68] By 1776 Lady Temple was not surprisingly 'low spirited',[69] and on her death the following year her husband was 'much dejected, more so even then I expected', according to his nephew.[70] Nevertheless he again rallied to the great challenge and later that year wrote to William Pitt: 'This same Hill of Stowe, on which we have spent our Happiest days perhaps, though not your most glorious, is so changed, that you would scarce know it again.'[71] Even in his last hours, in September 1779, 'his deliberations turned solely upon his buildings'.[72] He had in fact, after almost nine years, outlived the completion of the south front by just five months. 'Long Legs' or 'Squire Gawky', now a lonely widower, isolated in an unfinished palace amid a vast garden and park, met his end after being 'thrown out of a chaise on a heap of bricks' while driving at Stowe.[73]

5

The first Marquess and the first Duke

Under the Marquess of Buckingham, Earl Temple's nephew and successor, Stowe reached the height of its splendour. George Grenville had many advantages; his early stammer was corrected by Sheridan's father, and he went on to be a fine orator. When his father, who had been prime minister, died in 1770, George's uncle at Stowe became his guardian. In 1774 he undertook the Grand Tour and the next year married Mary Nugent, an Irish Catholic heiress aged 16 and supposedly with £14,000 per annum. In 1779, aged 26, he inherited Stowe, but he was busy elsewhere for most of the next ten years.

In politics he did not achieve his greatest ambitions. Although he was twice Lord Lieutenant of Ireland (1782–83, 1787–89), and was created Marquess of Buckingham in 1784, he had hoped for a dukedom. He therefore resigned as secretary of state in protest after only three days. In contrast his cousin, William Pitt the Younger, became prime minister in 1783 aged 24, and was succeeded on his death in office during his second ministry in 1806 by the youngest Grenville brother, William. The third brother, Thomas, was an ambassador and bibliophile. Their income was vast, much of it public money; William Cobbett reckoned that the three brothers received some £900,000 from the state. But their income shrank when they lost office, and even the rent rolls of a substantial estate could not support Buckingham's ambitious plans for Stowe.

His biggest changes were to the grand approaches. Before 1797, he realigned the end of the main drive at an angle to the house, thus demolishing Nelson's Seat, and moved the statue of King George I, which Cobham had placed to dominate the western approach to the house, to its present position. He spent large sums on enlarging the estate, planting the Oxford Avenue in 1804 along the south-eastern approach toward the Boycott Pavilions, but shortage of money probably made him abandon the plan to continue it in a direct line further south-east to Tingewick. On either side of Lord Temple's

The Temple Family, 1780–82, oil on canvas, Sir Joshua Reynolds's portrait of the first Marquess and Marchioness of Buckingham, with their young son, later the first Duke, and a black servant. Lady Buckingham was a skilled musician and artist – she studied under Reynolds – and had an impish sense of humour

Corinthian Arch on the Grand Avenue approach from Buckingham, he added the two milliary (milestone) columns, and at the southern end of the Grand Avenue he built the Barracks in 1802 and the two Buckingham Lodges in about 1805.

The first Marquess added the two milestone columns on either side of Temple's Corinthian Arch

Within the garden the Marquess mainly restricted himself to repairs and embellishments, no doubt partly for financial reasons, since by 1804 money was said to be running short. He re-used a marble chimneypiece, perhaps from the house, for the Seasons Fountain, one of the last additions to the garden, probably made by 1805 for the visit of the Prince of Wales, and named after James Thomson's popular long poem *The Seasons* (1746). With the help of the Italian architect Vincenzo Valdrè, he strengthened the Cobham Monument in 1792 and redecorated the Queen's Temple in 1790. Below the south front he installed the stone balustrade in 1790 with its pair of flower gardens. In 1792–94 he repaired the church of St Mary and introduced classical ceilings inside the house. As a solace after his wife's death in 1812, the Marquess enlarged the garden, enclosing 28 acres of the park east of the Cobham Monument. He also finished his uncle's steady clearance of some of Lord Cobham's garden buildings, such as the Pebble Rotondo, St Augustine's Cave and the visible remains of the Egyptian Pyramid designed by Vanbrugh (all now gone). By now Buckingham must have agreed with Thomas Jefferson, future US president and then minister to France, who in 1786 called the garden the 'pleasure grounds', regarding Stowe primarily as a place of entertainment. Buckingham had the Menagerie built *c.*1781 near the lower flower garden, as a refuge for his wife from the crowds of visitors in the house, doubtless employing Valdrè to decorate the central circular room. Lady Buckingham naturalised the appearance of Dido's Cave, near the Rotondo, and partially buried the Grotto, originally designed by

Kent to stand entirely above ground in the Elysian Fields. In the back of the Orangery she founded a village school.

As with his uncle, politics remained important to Buckingham. In March 1789 he was still in Ireland, his position as lord lieutenant dependent on George III remaining king without the Prince of Wales as regent. Lady Buckingham, therefore, celebrated the King's recovery from madness by illuminating the north front at Stowe 'very thoroughly' and roasting a whole ox, which was distributed to 2000 people. She admitted that this was her brother-in-law's idea, but was pleased that 'all the quality of Buckingham came to see it'.[74] The following year the interior of the Queen's Temple was decorated with reliefs by sculptor Charles Peart, recording the success of Queen Charlotte's dedicated nursing of her husband.

There were also large family celebrations, such as those recorded by Betsey Fremantle from Swanbourne in the Wynne diaries from 1797. Lady Buckingham's birthday was celebrated by the tenants' ball and dinner for 300 poor folk, while her younger son, Lord George, had a birthday party for 'sixty poor children that can read'. The younger house guests amused themselves with antics like dressing up as gipsies; then, going outside, 'they enraged the gardeners'.[75] The Wynne sisters were also to be found skating on the lakes or, in warmer seasons, rowing with the librarian Dr O'Connor; once they 'almost drowned him'.[76] Sometimes Lord Buckingham, and more often his wife, joined in the fun. On 1 January, 1810, Lord George Grenville's 21st birthday was celebrated by a lunch for nearly 1000 poor people from 12 neighbouring parishes, in thatched booths near the north front. His health was drunk in plenty of Stowe beer, and sports and fireworks followed.

During his last 15 years at Stowe, the Marquess spent much of his time entertaining. At Christmas 1799, Thomas Grenville wrote: 'Stowe is alternately filling and emptying, or rather is successively filling without emptying. The weather is still fine enough for exercise, and when I do not walk I collate Homer all morning and play at back-gammon all evening.'[77] Earlier that year there was talk of King George III visiting to review the Volunteers. Many exiled French royalty stayed at Stowe during the first decade of the nineteenth century. The most famous of these visits was in January 1808, when Louis XVIII and seven relatives planted four clumps of eight oaks near the Keeper's Lodge, renamed the Bourbon Tower in their honour. Lady Buckingham escorted the King, who was carried in the garden chair owing to his 'immense corpulency'. In fact most of the planting was done by the labourers, who paraded past the house in 'a ludicrous Procession, some with Spades, forks, or rakes, some driving wheelbarrows … the Band playing before them';[78] they then drank the King's health in the wine and ale he provided.

The Seasons Fountain, one of the last additions to the garden, was made from a re-used marble chimneypiece

Dido's Cave, part of
Cobham's political
garden, was naturalised
by Lady Buckingham

In August 1805 the Prince of Wales, later George IV, and his
brother, the Duke of Clarence, later King William IV, stayed at Stowe.
After an 11am breakfast, the Prince walked with Lady Buckingham to
the Flower Garden 'and was drove by her in the Garden Chair'.[79]
On the Friday evening they had supper in the Grotto, while the
Knyvetts sang catches and glees. Betsey Fremantle 'sat snug in the
grotto by Charles Fox'.[80] 118 fine drawings by Nattes record the
grounds at this time.

The Marquess was the first member of his family to become heavily
involved in supporting both the Royal Buckinghamshire Militia and the
Royal Buckinghamshire Yeomanry. The latter was a cavalry regiment,
founded in 1794 in response to the national threat posed by the French
Revolution, which remained mainly based at Stowe until World War I
and was kept by the family virtually as their private army. For over a
century from 1803, the yeomanry reviews and races were annual events
in Stowe Park. 'All the neighbourhood was there,' Betsey Fremantle
recorded, 'and the sight of the ground and the concourse of people
was charming.'[81]

Buckingham's elder son Richard shared his father's military
interests and also began a career in politics. He was an undistinguished
joint paymaster-general and deputy president of the Board of Trade
in 1806–7, when his uncle, Lord Grenville, was prime minister.
Nevertheless in 1822 he finally achieved the family's long-standing
ambition of a dukedom, becoming the first Duke of Buckingham
and Chandos. In doing so, however, he had to abandon his family's
long-held Whig principles, so clearly illustrated in Lord Cobham's first
landscaping work at Stowe, and accept the Tory whip in Parliament.
This, together with the 1832 Reform Act, which substantially enlarged
the electorate and swept away the rotten boroughs like Buckingham and
St Mawes, ended the Grenville family's domination of national politics
for the previous half-century.

The first Duke added greatly to the collections in Stowe House
through his marriage in 1796 at the age of 20 to Anna Eliza Brydges,
then aged only 16; the marriage had been arranged ten years before in

Bath. As the heiress of the last Duke of Chandos, she brought considerable wealth and the Chandos name. The dispersal of many great continental collections following the French Revolution provided further scope for the Duke's acquisitiveness. He was one of the buyers at the Orléans sales in 1798 and continued to buy paintings for the next 20 years, also amassing large collections of engravings and books, commissioning a lavish porcelain service and indulging his scientific and archaeological interests on a massive scale.

Extravagance came naturally to him; when he shut up Stowe to save costs in 1827, he instead spent two years on his yacht, touring the Mediterranean and collecting antiquities. He was reputedly the heaviest man ever to be carried up Mount Vesuvius. His Italian purchases comprised 18 crates of statuary and a further 30 large packages containing works of art. His personal expenditure was also out of control; in October 1820 he had bought 84 hats for £180. He made few economies until they were forced upon him, with the sales of Stowe property that started in 1833, and he continued misguidedly to borrow

The Cobham Monument and Queen's Temple in 1805; ink and wash drawing by J.C.Nattes

money in order to buy land which yielded a lower rate of return than the interest charged on the loan.

The dukedom was not the family's only ambition. They had also long coveted the neighbouring Lamport estate, comprising the land east of the Palladian Bridge and rising up to the Gothic Temple, which the first Duke eventually purchased in 1826. He was thus the last of the family to extend the garden, enclosing 17 additional acres on the south-eastern corner. He enlarged the Octagon Lake, and the head gardener, James Brown, added a small cascade below a picturesque rock and water garden east of the Palladian Bridge. In 1831 the garden designer J.C.Loudon noted that the garden had been greatly improved since 1806 by Brown, 'who may justly be said to have received the mantle of his great namesake and predecessor in the same garden'.[82] The first Duke made some further minor changes. In 1814, within a year of inheriting Stowe, he erected the Gothic Cross to the south of the church (now gone), perhaps in memory of his mother, and added the Evergreen Walk nearby, together with an inscription to his mother at Dido's Cave and an urn in memory of his father. Like his father, he was reluctant to remove many buildings, despite repeated criticism of the excessive number; the German nobleman, traveller and diarist Prince Pückler-Müskau wrote in 1828: 'It is so overcrowded with temples of all kinds that the greatest improvement that could be carried out here would consist in pulling down about ten or twelve of them.'[83]

In the 1820s the Duke turned part of the Menagerie into a museum and laid out the upper and lower flower gardens with a new fountain nearby. As his portly physique indicated, he valued his kitchen gardens highly and had originally brought in Brown to superintend these, only later putting him in charge of the pleasure grounds. Despite his growing financial problems, he insisted on repairing the Temple of Venus in 1827–28. He also demanded that rhododendrons be planted in the Alder valley and, in 1831, a new American border. That year, however, Loudon reported that the garden was not kept as before: 'the number of hands being yearly lessened. In new and rare plants, trees, and shrubs, the grounds are not keeping pace with the nurseries.'[84]

The first Duke was probably responsible for the new deer-park to the south-west of the garden. This formed a picturesque setting for his new Queen's Drive and its two New Ponds of c.1821.

The Queen's Temple today

Richard, Earl Temple, later first Duke of Buckingham and Chandos, hand-coloured etching by Robert Dighton, 1811

The old park to the north was thus freed for cavalry drill practice and a cannon range. He extended the private carriage drive north to Silverstone, building the present pair of stone lodges where it joins the main road. He also probably erected the Chackmore Fountain beside the Grand Avenue in 1831 (demolished in the late 1950s).

There were relatively few jamborees at Stowe during the first Duke's time, partly because of his growing financial troubles, and partly because his wife preferred to live at Avington in Hampshire. Nevertheless on a snowy February day in 1818, his son's 21st birthday was celebrated in the now customary way, with thatched booths and an ox roast on the north lawn. Again in June 1824, true to his extravagant nature, the 'Stowe Junket' at his grandson's baptism may have been the largest ever; over 190 guests stayed in the house alone and many more were lodged in Buckingham for the week, while a ball for 1100 was held in an ordnance tent sent by the Duke of Wellington.

6

Decline and fall

Richard Plantagenet Temple-Nugent-Brydges-Chandos-Grenville, second Duke of Buckingham from 1839, took the royal element of his name from his mother's family. With a personal income of £14,000, he could have afforded to live in reasonable state, but he inherited and developed the first Duke's extravagant tastes, and combined a talent for embezzlement with a fatal plausibility that made many of his friends easy victims. He went to Oxford but did not take a degree, instead entering politics and becoming leader of the landed Conservatives in the House of Commons from 1816. He sponsored the Chandos clause, an extension of the franchise added to the 1832 Reform Bill, earning the title of 'the Farmers' Friend', and resigned as lord privy seal in 1842. Expense was no object; after the house at Wotton was burnt down in 1820, it was rebuilt by leading architect Sir John Soane. The Duke's main joy, as Jackson's portrait implies, was the Buckinghamshire Yeomanry. He probably replaced the dark blue and gold of Stowe's old livery, still the school's colours, with the Grenville green of the new yeomanry uniforms, for which he paid. At his son's baptism in 1824, his great-aunt complained that he was much more concerned with his yeomanry than his heir; in fact the following year he gave away the gilt christening cup to a private, for winning a horse race in the park. Fittingly, his monument at Stowe is the obelisk erected by his yeomanry in the old Drill Park near the Bourbon Tower.

Once he inherited Stowe in 1839, the second Duke sold a thousand pictures, but this was merely to make room for further acquisitions. He also succeeded in deceiving his creditors long enough to undertake a vast programme of repairs to the house and garden buildings in the next five years. With Edward Blore as architect, he re-sited many of the smaller monuments and statues. He was particularly fond of stone urns and vases, erecting monuments to both his parents and to the Queen of Hanover. He also spent vast sums on rebuilding much of the kitchen garden in nearby Dadford. To strengthen security at the garden

The Marquess of Chandos, later the second Duke, painted by John Jackson in 1829; he is wearing his Grenville green Hussar uniform as commander of the Buckinghamshire Yeomanry

entrances, he constructed the Garden, Lamport and Water Stratford
Lodges, and employed several army pensioners as gatekeepers. He
had little understanding of landscape gardening and erected fences and
walls where he fancied, enclosing his father's picturesque Lamport or
Japanese gardens with a wire fence, to keep the foxes away from his
pheasants and exotic birds. He took great joy in turning the Bourbon
Tower into a mock fort and creating the cannon and rifle range
close by.

Although the second Duke was keen to deter unwanted visitors,
he was equally anxious to attract royalty to Stowe. Thus in January
1840 there was a visit by the Duke of Cambridge, an uncle of Queen
Victoria, and his son, Prince George. In August that year William
IV's widow, the Dowager Queen Adelaide, visited, together with the
Archbishop of Canterbury. Disraeli understood that 'the outdoor part,
as far as triumphal arches, processions, crowds in the gardens, &c, was
very successful.'[85] The King of Hanover and the Duchess of Gloucester
came in 1843. The following year the Duke laid on a grand gala for his
son's coming-of-age, although this was aimed at persuading him to sign
over his destined inheritance to his spendthrift father. The climax came
in January 1845, when his friend Robert Peel, the prime minister,
persuaded Queen Victoria and Prince Albert to stay at Stowe. The
Duke was already in debt to the staggering sum of over £1 million, but
he borrowed yet more to cram his house with new furniture. The pair
of oak and cedar trees outside the Temple of Concord and Victory is
the only obvious reminder of this visit. He hoped to turn the temple's
interior into a commemorative shrine, but his impending ruin prevented
its completion.

In August 1847 the Duke's effects were seized by bailiffs acting for
a cartel of his creditors, and he fled abroad. His affairs were taken over
by trustees, in consultation with his son, the 24-year-old Marquess of

Chandos, who was suddenly aware that his father had for several years been making fraudulent attempts on his inheritance.

In March 1848 most of the outlying parts of the estate, in Ireland, Hampshire and London, were sold, but the market was soon flooded and most of it went very cheaply. Likewise, the great sale of the contents by Christie's, which lasted for 40 days from 15 August to 7 October 1848, raised only £75,400. Writing in *The Times* on 14 August, the historian Thomas Babington Macaulay lamented:

During the past week the British public has been admitted to a spectacle of a painfully interesting and gravely historical import. One of the most splendid abodes of our almost regal aristocracy has thrown open its portals to an endless succession of visitors, who from morning to night have flowed in an uninterrupted stream from room to room, and floor to floor – not to enjoy the hospitality of the lord, or to congratulate him on his countless treasures of art, but to see an ancient family ruined, their place marked for destruction, and its contents scattered to the four winds of Heaven. We are only saying what is notorious … that the Most Noble and Puissant Prince, his Grace the Duke of Buckingham and Chandos, is at this moment an absolutely ruined and destitute man. … Stowe is no more.

What now seems most remarkable about the catastrophic events of 1848 is that they did not in fact mark the end of the family at Stowe. By 1861, when the second Duke died in the Great Western Hotel at Paddington ('from the splendour of a prince to the grade of a lodger'), his son Richard had recovered the family's affairs sufficiently to return to live at Stowe. In 1865 Disraeli could write that 'the flag waves once again over Stowe, which no one expected'.[86]

Since 1847, the future third Duke and his agent Thomas Beards had executed a policy of retrenchment over the whole estate, while still

The pair of trees, oak and cedar, outside the Temple of Concord and Victory were planted during Queen Victoria's visit

The Temple of Ancient
Virtue at the time of the
Stowe sale in 1848

preserving its Buckinghamshire core of 10,000 acres. The house was
mothballed, the garden staff reduced from 40 to four and much of the
garden left for grazing, while the garden buildings received minimal
maintenance. From 1848 onwards, not just the outlying woods, but all
but one of the great avenues was sold for timber.

From the 1860s the accounts show expenditure on new furnishings
for the house, and on repairs to the garden buildings. The Palladian
Bridge was overhauled, the Temple of Friendship consolidated, and the
Bell Gate refurbished and reopened to admit visitors to the gardens.
The garden staff was restored to some 30 men, and new plantings
undertaken, in particular cedars along Pegg's Terrace on the southern
edge of the garden, and sequoias on the Paddock Course Walk to the
north of the Grecian Valley. The upper and lower flower gardens
established by the first Marquess were also restored. The museum by
the lower flower garden was restocked with fresh curiosities, such as
'a fine specimen of the sacred bull of the Hindoos', a granite sculpture
excavated by the Duke while serving as governor of Madras from
1874 to 1880.

The third Duke's achievement in rescuing Stowe was in its way as
great as the work of those who created it, but he could never entirely
recover the status of the family. On his death in 1889 he left no male
heir, despite having married for the second time four years previously,
and the dukedom became extinct after only 67 years. Stowe passed
to his eldest daughter, Mary, Lady Morgan-Grenville, who also
inherited the title Lady Kinloss, but she had no use for the house
and considered selling.

The widowed Lady Kinloss returned for a short while to Stowe
in 1901, after a brief and bizarre interlude of five years in which it
had served as the court of the Comte de Paris, exiled claimant to the
French crown, who had previously been accommodated at Claremont
and Whittlebury.

In 1908 the coming-of-age of Richard, Master of Kinloss, grandson of the third Duke and heir to Stowe, was marked with celebrations that recalled the great fêtes of the early nineteenth century, with 400 tenants seated for lunch. But the resemblance was entirely superficial. The Master of Kinloss was killed in the first few months of World War I. When peace returned, his younger brother put the Stowe estate on the market and it was sold in July 1921, with some of the contents and garden statuary, to Mr Harry Shaw of Beenham Court, near Newbury, for £50,000. Most of the remaining contents and statuary were sold on in the following year.

The Temple of Ancient Virtue today

7

Recovery

Our immediate and worst forebodings regarding Stowe have been most happily dispelled by the generous intervention of Mr Shaw of Beenham Court. ... Certainly there are few places better worth while preserving or better suited for public delight and education. Properly arranged and wisely administered Stowe might become a great cultural centre.
CLOUGH WILLIAMS-ELLIS, *The Spectator*, 23 July 1921

As a result of this article, Clough Williams-Ellis found himself appointed as architect to the governing body of Stowe School, which purchased the house and garden from Mr Shaw in October 1922. His initial task was to adapt the main body of the house to form classrooms and dormitories; the school received its first pupils in May 1923. The quality of the buildings and landscape was central to the educational ideals of Stowe's first headmaster, J.F.Roxburgh, who was appointed at the age of 35 and very swiftly established its reputation: 'If we do not fail in our purpose,' he wrote, 'every boy who goes out from Stowe will know beauty when he sees it all the rest of his life.'[87] Williams-Ellis and other architects, including Sir Robert Lorimer, designed some of the first of the ancillary buildings. Initially most of these were well integrated with the house and its landscape, but Williams-Ellis's Chatham House (1924–25) introduced a discordant style and material (red brick) into the views from the Rotondo and Temple of Venus, and the building of the school chapel to Lorimer's designs in 1928 involved the demolition of Vanbrugh's Temple of Bacchus. Worse, the chapel itself incorporated eighteenth-century fittings removed from the chapel in the house, and 16 of the Ionic columns from the peristyle of the Temple of Concord and Victory.

But against this can be set the repairs undertaken from an early stage in the school's history to other garden buildings, notably the Queen's Temple, which was restored in 1933–34 under Fielding Dodd (with donations from the first generation of Old Stoics) and became part of the music department. In the course of the 1950s and 1960s, the school carried out repairs to ten further buildings and monuments,

including the Cobham Monument after it had been struck by lightning in 1957. The Gothic Temple and the eastern Boycott Pavilion became habitable, the former as one of the projects of the Landmark Trust.

The school single-handedly maintained the garden for 30 years before it was officially recognised that the preservation of the Stowe landscape was a national responsibility. In 1954 the newly formed Historic Buildings Council made its first grants for the upkeep of garden buildings, supporting repairs at Stowe and at Castle Howard. In order to raise the funds necessary to match these grants independently of the school's education resources, the Stowe Landscape Committee was re-formed in 1964, with Sir Ralph Verney as its chairman, and members including architectural historians Christopher Hussey and Howard Colvin, poet and artist Laurence Whistler, and town planner Lord Holford. The committee appointed the architect Hugh Creighton to report on the condition of the buildings, and to draw up a ten-year plan for repairs. The aim of the plan, as he put it, was 'emphatically not to restore the buildings to their pristine condition nor attempt to

[above]
The Temple of Concord and Victory required major conservation

[left]
Detail of the Chinese House before restoration

undo the work of 200 years. It is, in general, to make them structurally sound in their present state, to keep out the weather, and to arrest further deterioration.'[88]

In 1967 the governors entered into a restrictive covenant with the National Trust in order to secure the long-term future of the core of the garden. The replanting of the avenues and other historic plantings was begun with the help of John Workman, the National Trust's forestry adviser, and much of the practical work was undertaken by schoolboys supervised by George Clarke, who taught at Stowe from 1950 until 1985, and whose research with Michael Gibbon into the history of Stowe was published in a series of definitive articles in the school magazine, *The Stoic*, from 1967 to 1977.

When Creighton prepared a second report in 1983, however, it became clear that the rate at which the landscape committee had been able to carry out repairs was far outstripped by the pace of dilapidation. Simply to make holding repairs to three of the buildings, the Temple of Ancient Virtue, the Corinthian Arch and the Temple of Concord, all of which had received attention in the past 20 years, now required expenditure of £600,000. In 1986 a group of Old Stoics promoted the formation of a new body, the Stowe Garden Buildings Trust, in order to raise the necessary funds, but to many the preservation of Lord Cobham's creation had come to seem an impossible task.

The possibility that the National Trust might extend its role at Stowe emerged in 1989, when an anonymous benefactor offered to contribute £1.8 million, if the Trust were to assume ownership of the garden and its buildings. This was swiftly followed by offers of support from English Heritage and the National Heritage Memorial Fund, and the school governors formally conveyed the garden to the National Trust in 1990. For the first time since 1848, it became possible to plan a comprehensive restoration of the garden and its buildings, and, with the provision of an endowment by the NHMF, the long-term future of the landscape now seems secure.

In parallel with the National Trust's work in the gardens, the Stowe House Preservation Trust (SHPT) was created in 1997 to raise funds for and manage the restoration of the main mansion, and to increase public access to the state rooms. To date, it has achieved three phases out of a six-phase restoration plan costing some £30m. The exterior of the house has now been secured and the restoration of the state room interiors is well underway. With support from the World Monument Fund (Britain), Country Houses Foundation, the National Memorial Fund, English Heritage, the Heritage Lottery Fund and many other generous private donors, SHPT continues its tireless work of restoring the magnificent eighteenth-century ducal palace, which is open to the public in both termtime and holidays.

Carving a new capital for the Temple of Concord and Victory

[overleaf]
Priority has been given to maintaining the main views and axes unchanged

[left]
The circle of Saxon Deities has been re-assembled

[right]
Copy of one of the original figures in the Temple of Ancient Virtue

The National Trust's first task as owners was to carry out a thorough survey so that the work of restoration could be properly planned. Individual trees, woodland boundaries, built structures, contours, roads and paths, fences, lakes and streams were all plotted on an overall plan; to this were added an inventory of woody plants, an assessment of biological interest, and an archaeological survey, which identified more than 90 'sites' within the garden (including the 32 standing buildings).

The Stowe papers are preserved in the Huntington Library, California, and were consulted under the guidance of George Clarke, first chairman of the advisory committee jointly constituted by the school and the National Trust to direct restoration. The Stowe Advisory Panel is now the principal consultation body for the restoration of house and garden.

Based on the results of the survey compiled by its gardens adviser, Mike Calnan, the Trust devised a conservation plan in which the objectives for the restoration were set out. The first principle was to ensure the preservation of built or planted features that were meant as additions to the design, leaving the future of others to be decided on their merits. Another was the perpetuation of the main views and axes, which have not essentially changed since 1800. While gardens are continuously changing processes rather than static objects, and any attempt to freeze the Stowe landscape at a particular date would fail, it has been established that very little of what survives today was begun after the garden and park were accurately mapped in 1843. This huge map is therefore of considerable importance in assessing the form of a plantation or the course of a path. In general, alterations up to this period are being conserved, but in some instances, where areas of the garden matured earlier, restoration will recapture the style of that time.

The extent to which nature had begun to triumph over art was nowhere more evident than in the condition of the lakes, and their clearance was the Trust's first large-scale operation. It had become possible in places to walk across what were originally wide stretches of water. Under head gardener Frank Thomson, the Alder River and

Worthies River, the Octagon Lake and Palladian River, the Eleven-Acre and Copper Bottom Lakes, and finally the Oxford Water were dredged, yielding a total of 320,000 tonnes of silt.

The problem of over-mature trees is often encountered in the restoration of old gardens; at Stowe the tree population shows a mixture of ages, with the smallest proportion surviving from the eighteenth century, largely because of the third Duke's need to maximise his income from timber. Since 1989 the Trust has felled a number of commercial softwood plantings (for instance, a spruce plantation obscuring the site of the Saxon Deities), thinned other areas, and replanted 20,000 trees and shrubs. The re-establishment of paths combines archaeology with the study of plans. In the first few years of the project these were surfaced with chippings from the woodland thinnings, but more recently with gravel dug from the Stowe pits. The National Trust employs eight full-time gardeners and also has a growing team of volunteers, as well as visits from a number of corporate teams who come on team-building days

The removal of almost all of the statuary from the garden in 1848 and 1921–22 (well over a hundred pieces) stripped away the complex meanings and associations so carefully devised by Lord Cobham.

The National Trust has carried out holding works on the Palladian Bridge

Major repairs have been made to the Conduit House

However, with the encouragement and co-operation of their present owners, the Trust has begun to reintroduce many of the statues in the form of casts. Copies of the four Virtuous Greeks have thus been returned to their niches in the Temple of Ancient Virtue, and the circle of the Saxon Deities, with the exception of Thuner, has been re-assembled in the Wick Quarter.

The condition of the garden buildings was reassessed in 1989–90 by Peter Inskip, who then proposed a sequence of campaigns of repair. Their condition varied, but almost all of them required attention, and while progress has been made, it will take some years yet to finish the task. The Trust's fundamental policy is to conserve as much as possible of the original fabric of each temple or monument. Holding works have been carried out to the Temple of Friendship and the Palladian Bridge, and major work is also required on the Bourbon Tower and East Boycott Pavilion. The largest tasks so far have been the repairs to the Grenville Column, the Temple of Ancient Virtue, the Oxford Gates and Lodges, the Temples of Venus and Concord and Victory, the Rotondo and Dido's Cave, the Cobham Monument and the Fane of Pastoral Poetry, General Wolfe's Obelisk, the Conduit House, the Lake Pavilions and, most recently, the Grotto. The roof of the Temple of Ancient Virtue was found to be bearing unequally on the Ionic peristyle, and the surrounding ground levels were much altered. A concrete ring-beam now supports the dome, and the renders have been completed using the constituents of the original material.

Kent's original domes to the pavilions of the Temple of Venus had already subsided by 1827–28, when the first Duke of Buckingham replaced them with pitched lead roofs. At about the same time the door openings were enlarged, the south-facing windows blocked up, and what was left of the original decoration obscured by new paint. In the twentieth century the coved ceiling collapsed and was removed. Faced with so severely damaged a building, the Stowe Advisory Committee approved a proposal to restore as much of Kent's original design as could reliably be reconstructed. Sadly, this could not include the murals by Venetian painter Francesco Sleter, of which only a single hand and part of the branch of a tree survived.

The Temple of Concord had been on death row for decades, and by the early 1980s there seemed little point in spending anything further on keeping the roof watertight. With the renewed commitment of English Heritage and the assistance of private benefactors, however, it has since been possible to reroof the building entirely, to carve and reinstate 16 new columns (the originals remain in Lorimer's chapel, which is itself now a listed building), to restore the interior and the stucco of the external walls, and to reinstate sculpture to the roof, at a cost of £1.3 million. In 1995 the National Trust was able to purchase the 320 acres of the Home Farm which lie immediately to the north of the garden, with the help of funds from the National Lottery distributed by the Heritage Lottery Fund.

The Temple of Concord and Victory, focus of major restoration work

The New Inn in 1805–09; ink and wash drawing by J.C.Nattes

The New Inn before restoration; after extensive work by the National Trust, it has now resumed its original purpose as a place of welcome for visitors

In 2005 the National Trust acquired the New Inn, which had been built in 1717 by Lord Cobham to accommodate visitors to the garden, but which had long since been converted to agricultural use and had fallen into dereliction. The Trust carefully restored this fine example of an early eighteenth-century posting inn, retaining its courtyard of stables, coach-house, kitchen, brew-house and laundry, together with the later farm buildings. This project has enabled the Trust to recreate the traditional entrance to Stowe as planned by Cobham, so that visitors can at last experience the gardens as they were meant to be seen. Opened in summer 2011, this new Visitor Centre also provides a welcome befitting the magnificence of Stowe.

8

The fame of Stowe

Alexander Pope called Stowe 'a work to wonder at'.[89] Like most eighteenth-century visitors, he was impressed by the size, splendour and variety of the gardens and their unusual abundance of ornamental buildings – 'decorations', remarked the Swedish garden architect F.M.Piper in 1779, 'of a dimension, size and variety that betray a desire to gain renown and to exceed all others in point of expense and magnitude'.[90] Stowe was a microcosm of landscape and building and was, asserted Thomas Whately in 1770, 'like one of those places celebrated in antiquity … the resort of distant nations and the object of veneration to half the heathen world'.[91]

Despite Stowe's immense popularity, it is difficult to calculate the extent of the garden's influence, and to differentiate it from that of other important English landscape gardens of the day. Claremont, Richmond, Chiswick and Stourhead all had features in common with Stowe, and several smaller gardens, such as Woburn Farm, Painshill and The Leasowes, approached it in influence and reputation. With the exception of Kew, however, no other English garden of the eighteenth century could rival the number, scale and complex iconography of the ornamental garden buildings at Stowe. Moreover, many of these structures were by celebrated architects, giving Stowe a distinct architectural emphasis, which often overshadowed the significance of the landscape and planting.

Soon after Lord Cobham began work on the gardens, he opened them to the curious, building the New Inn on the margins of the garden in 1717 to accommodate visitors. Stowe was also the subject of the first guidebook, by Benton Seeley, to any country house garden in England. Public curiosity was fuelled further by other publications – poetic tributes such as Gilbert West's *Stowe* (1732) or prose descriptions like those found in Samuel Richardson's edition of Defoe's *A Tour thro' the Whole Island of Great Britain* (1742).

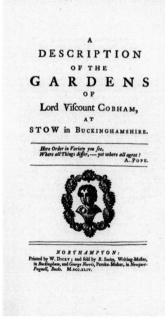

A
DESCRIPTION
OF THE
GARDENS
OF
Lord Viſcount COBHAM,
AT
STOW in BUCKINGHAMSHIRE.

Here Order in Variety you see,
Where all Things differ, — yet where all agree!
A. POPE.

NORTHAMPTON:
Printed by W. DICEY; and ſold by B. Seeley, Writing-Maſter, in Buckingham, and George Norris, Peruke-Maker, in Newport-Pagnell, Bucks. M.DCC.XLIV.

[above]
The title page from the first edition of Benton Seeley's Stowe guidebook (1744), which helped to spread the fame of the garden

[right]
Cobham's radical Gothic Temple, with the Palladian Bridge in the foreground; the Temple had no close imitators

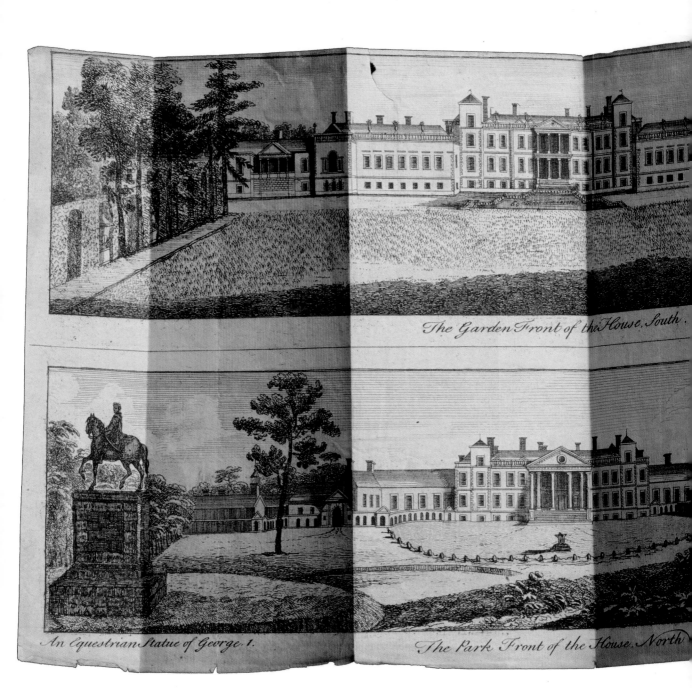

The Garden Front of the House, South.

An Equestrian Statue of George. I.

The Park Front of the House, North

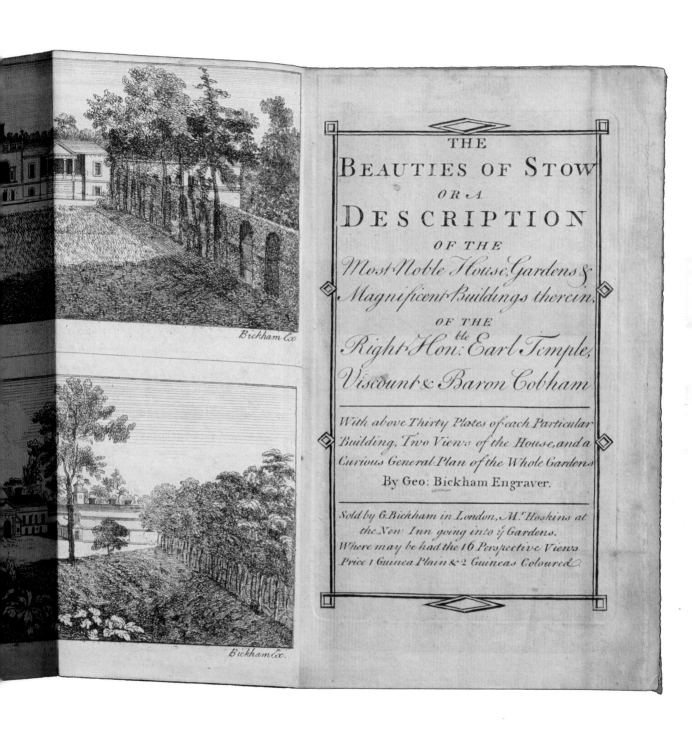

THE

BEAUTIES OF STOW

OR A

DESCRIPTION

OF THE

Most Noble House, Gardens &
Magnificent Buildings therein,

OF THE

Right Hon: ble Earl Temple,

Viscount & Baron Cobham

With above Thirty Plates of each Particular
Building, Two Views of the House, and a
Curious General Plan of the Whole Gardens
By Geo: Bickham Engraver.

Sold by G.Bickham in London, Mr.Hoskins at
the New Inn going into ÿ Gardens.
Where may be had the 16 Perspective Views
Price 1 Guinea Plain & 2 Guineas Coloured

Bickham Ex

Bickham Ex.

George Bickham's
The Beauties of Stow
(1753) was produced
in competition with
Seeley's guidebooks

From 1750 these published descriptions were supplemented by
illustrations of the gardens, although they were by no means always
accurate or up-to-date. Cobham's formal gardens were known from
a handsome series of engraved views by Jacques Rigaud, published in
1739, but these had been drawn in 1733–34 and depicted only its formal
'Bridgmannick' elements and none of Kent's Arcadian incursions. Even
the crude 'cuts' of the garden buildings from Seeley and Bickham's
guidebooks showed little of their landscape context. Stowe was never
the subject of a serious architectural publication like Sir William
Chambers's *Plans … of the Gardens and Buildings at Kew* (1763) and
perhaps even more regrettably, none of Nattes's watercolour views
of the gardens at around their zenith in 1805–09 (see p.59) was ever
engraved. The fame of Stowe was well established by 1724, having
already 'gained the reputation of being the finest seat in England'.[92]
Even at this early date it was unrivalled for its unusual garden buildings,
some of which were imitated elsewhere. Vanbrugh's Rotondo (1720–21)
was copied at Hall Barn (1725) and at Studley Royal (c.1728–32). His
Pyramid (1724; now gone) inspired similar structures at Tring (c.1725)
and Castle Howard (1728; both also gone). No less influential than the
buildings was Bridgeman's ha-ha, a feature found in almost all large
landscape gardens later in the century.

Cobham's 'garden of exile' has affinities with those which consoled
other outcasts, notably the Tory Earl Bathurst at Cirencester Park (from
1714), the disgraced financier John Aislabie at Studley Royal (1720–42)
and the retired general James Dormer at Rousham (from 1737). Between
1739 and 1791, at the rival Yorkshire estates of Wentworth Castle and
Wentworth Woodhouse, an astonishing series of garden structures –
lookout towers, columns and obelisks – commemorated the divided
political allegiances of the estranged branches of one family. In an echo
of the Temple of British Worthies, Frederick, Prince of Wales set up
busts of King Alfred and the Black Prince in his garden at Carlton
House. He also planned a 'Mount Parnassus' for Kew on the model
of the Elysian Fields, but died before it could be completed.

Stowe's Arcadia intrigued rather than inspired most visitors.
Nothing came of an anonymous proposal of c.1735 to remodel the
gardens at Bovingdon House in Devon with a whole series of
monuments borrowed from Stowe, including a 'Dormitory', a
'Temple of the Worthies' and an 'Altar of the Saxon Gods'. Lord
Petre's unexecuted 1738 design for an ambitious garden for the Duke
of Norfolk at Worksop contained a Rotondo, a Temple of Ancient
Virtue and a Palladian Bridge, as well as a monster exedra doubtless
derived from the Temple of British Worthies. Curiously, the most
daring novelties erected at Stowe in the 1730s and 40s were also isolated
phenomena. The Chinese House (c.1738) was one of the first chinoiserie

**The Temple of Fame at
Studley Royal in
Yorkshire was inspired by
Vanbrugh's Rotondo at
Stowe**

garden buildings in Britain but had little influence on the next wave of Chinese structures, at Old Windsor, Shugborough and Kew. The most ambitious of all early Gothick garden buildings, the triangular Gothic Temple, also had no close imitators. Perhaps Stowe's most influential creation was 'Capability' Brown, who perfected his art and made his reputation there between 1741 and 1751. Subsequently, he worked on innumerable landscape gardens up and down the country, often being called upon to 'naturalise' earlier formal layouts, much as he had done at Stowe.

Many of the 'sacred landscapes' created by Brown and his followers in the second half of the eighteenth century can be compared to Stowe, including the temple-strewn gardens of West Wycombe and Wentworth Woodhouse. Indeed, it has been suggested that Sir Francis Dashwood planned features of West Wycombe in parody of his old enemy's gardens at Stowe. Friendlier family ties resulted in close parallels between Stowe and Hagley, the garden made by Lord Cobham's nephew George Lyttelton. Almost every feature at Hagley had a precursor at Stowe: the

The Chinese House, an early and isolated example of chinoiserie garden buildings in Britain

Carmontelle Giving the Keys of the Parc Monceau in Paris to the Duke of Chartres, oil on canvas, by Carmontelle (Louis Carrogis), showing the 'Wood of Tombs' in the Parc Monceau, the 'French Stowe'

'Grecian Temple' (1747; now the Temple of Concord and Victory) had a counterpart in Stuart's Temple of Theseus at Hagley (1758); Cobham's columns topped with statues of the Prince and Princess of Wales were answered by a similar column at Hagley, and both Stowe and Hagley had an Ionic Rotondo and a Palladian Bridge. Stowe Castle (before 1738) and the Keeper's Lodge (*c*.1741; now the Bourbon Tower) prefigured Hagley's Ruined Castle (1747). However, Lyttelton was also advised by William Shenstone of The Leasowes, and his gardens had a 'savage' aspect akin to the picturesque landscapes of Hawkstone and Hackfall. Many gardens which appear to be influenced by Stowe are in fact indebted to its rivals.

Temple's purification of the gardens, and the increasing maturity of Cobham's plantations, left Stowe at the height of its splendour and reputation. Yet because Temple primarily patronised foreign architects or sought advice from one of his aristocratic kinsmen, none of whom carried out much work elsewhere, Stowe was somewhat isolated architecturally. His ambitious plans for two grand commemorative buildings, a Mausoleum and a Rotondo, remained unrealised, although they may have influenced a contemporary political Valhalla at Wentworth Woodhouse, known as the Rockingham Mausoleum.

Distant echoes of Stowe can be found in countless gardens throughout northern Europe, but again direct links are curiously difficult to find. The French were particularly fascinated by Stowe, which was illustrated in George Le Rouge's *Détails de nouveaux jardins à la mode* (1776–88). Moreover, many Frenchmen came to see Stowe for themselves, descending on the gardens in such numbers that a guidebook entitled *Les Charmes de Stow* was brought out in 1748.

An evocation of Stowe can be found at the Parc Monceau, a celebrated *jardin anglais* laid out in 1773–78 for the anglophile duc de Chartres. Monceau was frequently compared to Stowe by French commentators and contained 'a quantity of curious things' – a minaret, pyramid, wood of tombs, Italian vineyard, military column, Turkish tent and a water-mill. However, it was also very like Kew and Painshill.

Reminders of Stowe occur in other French gardens of the period. At the Désert de Retz, François Racine de Monville created, from 1774, an extraordinary garden surrounding a house in the form of a shattered column, with exotic buildings like a Chinese house, a pyramid and a Gothic chapel. At Betz, designed by Hubert Robert and the duc d'Harcoult for the princesse de Monaco, the very names of the buildings – the Temple of Friendship and the Pavilion of Rest – suggest a conscious imitation of specific models from Stowe. Méréville, laid out from 1784 by F. J. Bélanger (who had visited England in 1777–78 and made drawings of Stowe) and Hubert Robert for the duc de Laborde, had a towering 'Colonne Triumphale', a monument to Captain Cook, and a peripteral temple resembling the Temple of Ancient Virtue. Other examples of the French mania for *jardins anglais* include those at Rambouillet, Bagatelle, Mauperthuis and around the Petit Trianon at Versailles, and, in perhaps its most extravagant and eccentric form, the gardens of the Folie Saint-James at Neuilly. Luxurious and 'loaded with incoherent and useless ornaments', almost all these gardens fell victim, like their owners, to the French Revolution.

In Germany the taste for English landscape gardens was taken up with perhaps even more enthusiasm than in France, thanks to influential publications such as C.C.L.Hirschfeld's *Theorie der Gartenkunst* (1779–85). In the 1760s Prince Franz von Anhalt-Dessau, accompanied by his architect and his gardener, made two visits to England and saw many important gardens, including Stowe. His gardens at Wörlitz, near Dessau, begun in 1770 and successively extended until 1800, contain more garden buildings than Stowe, including a synagogue, a Gothic house and a volcano, but none directly relates to structures at Stowe, and features like the Rousseau-Insel betray a clear debt to Ermenonville. A somewhat generalised English inspiration can be seen in the countless German landscape gardens of the second half of the eighteenth century, like those at Schwetzingen, remodelled for the Grand Duke of Baden from 1774 by Friedrich Ludwig von Sckell (who had studied in England), or Hohenheim, near Stuttgart.

In Sweden the English landscape manner was introduced by F.M.Piper, who had visited England in the 1770s and made drawings of Stowe and other English landscape gardens for his unpublished *Idea and Plan for an English Pleasure Park*. Piper subsequently promoted his ideas at a number of Swedish landscape gardens, including those at

Drottningholm and Haga. Gardens on the English model are also found in Hungary, notably in those laid out for members of the Esterházy family at Csákvár (1781–1800), Tata (from 1784) and Kismarton (from 1801). In Poland the style was promoted by the king, Stanislas Poniatowski, who had visited Stowe in 1754, and is exemplified by the garden-retreat of Arkadia, created by Princess Helena Radziwill and her architect Szymon Bogumil Zug.

But Stowe's greatest admirer was the Empress Catherine the Great of Russia, who was fascinated with English landscape gardens and sent her gardener Vasily Neelov to England in 1770–71 to 'visit all the notable gardens and, having seen them, lay out similar ones here'.[93] Neelov almost certainly saw Stowe during his six months' sojourn in England and spent the rest of his life recasting Catherine's pleasure grounds at Tsarskoe Selo and Peterhof in the English style. The former contains a sequence of Palladian Bridge, rostral column, Corinthian Arch and Pyramid all directly derived from Stowe. The 'Stoic' monuments at Tsarskoe Selo together comprise perhaps the most complete and studied evocation of the gardens anywhere. Unable to visit Stowe herself, the Empress was constantly reminded of the gardens and their significance: the celebrated Frog dinner service, commissioned by her from Wedgwood in 1773, has more views of Stowe than of any other garden.

Although southern Europe remained largely unaffected by the craze for English landscape gardens in the eighteenth century, the style was promoted in Italy in the early nineteenth century by Count Ercole Silva, author of *Dell' arte dei giardini inglesi* (1813), whose own gardens at Cinisello in Lombardy were described as 'the Leasowes or Stow of the Milanese'. Stowe found admirers across the Atlantic: Thomas Jefferson went to Stowe in 1786 and recalled it in his own garden at Monticello.

In the nineteenth century the gardens at Stowe gradually sank into decline, and contemporary opinion often echoed Prince Pückler-Müskau's criticisms (see p.60). Curiously, the very surfeit of ornaments he complained about became a characteristic of the grandest private and public pleasure grounds laid out later in the century. Comparison can be made between Stowe and the gardens Joseph Paxton designed for the Crystal Palace after it was moved to Sydenham, with their mixture of formal and informal elements and a host of novelties lurking in the shrubberies.

Denuded of its statuary by the sales of 1848 and 1921–22, Stowe in its ruin exerted perhaps a greater fascination than at any time in its history. The pleasing effects of time on the buildings and the full splendour of the overgrown planting coincided with a revival of appreciation of eighteenth-century architecture and landscape gardens. Despite its incongruity, the occupation of the great palace and its

The PALACE of MALPLAQUET

drawn by RAYMOND M'GRATH

Bird's-eye view of the gardens of the Palace of Malplaquet, a fictional Stowe, drawn by Raymond McGrath for the endpapers of T.H.White's *Mistress Masham's Repose*, 1947

pleasure grounds by Stowe School doubtless ensured its preservation far more effectively than had they remained in private ownership. The gardens, with their tangled undergrowth and decaying temples pressed into service as classrooms, boat-houses and tuck-shops, certainly had a potent influence on generations of young Stoics. Many may even regret the passing of their forlorn grandeur, celebrated in the paintings of John Piper and the photographs of Osvald Siren. The derelict gardens are also brilliantly evoked (as those of the fictional Malplaquet Palace) in T.H.White's novel, *Mistress Masham's Repose* (1947), and permeate the work of Rex and Laurence Whistler, the latter an Old Stoic. There is no twentieth-century equivalent to Stowe, although in recent times the influence of this decayed Arcadia can perhaps be found in the modern garden of inscriptions created by Ian Hamilton Finlay at Little Sparta.

Notes

1 The meaning of Stowe

1 John Martin Robinson, *Temples of Delight*, London, 1990, p.12

2 Mrs Paget Toynbee, ed., *The Letters of Horace Walpole*, Oxford, 1903, III, pp.180–1: letter to John Chute, 4 August 1753

2 Stowe before Viscount Cobham

3 E.F.Gay, 'The Rise of an English Country Family: Peter and John Temple, to 1603', *Huntington Library Quarterly*, 1938, pp.367–90

4 Cited in *Huntington Library Quarterly*, November 1942, p.291

5 Christopher Morris, ed., *The Illustrated Journeys of Celia Fiennes*, London, 1984, p.54

6 Letter from the steward William Chaplin to Sir Richard Temple, 18 March 1683, (Huntington Library); cited in John Harris, 'Wren's Work at Stowe', Letters, *Country Life*, CXXX, 3 August 1961, pp.254–5. Cited in George Clarke, 'Sir Richard Temple's House and Gardens', The History of Stowe IV, *The Stoic*, XXIII.2, no.135, March 1968, p.63

3 Viscount Cobham

7 Jonathan Swift, *The Journal to Stella*, 2007, p.310

8 William Congreve, letter to Duke of Newcastle (British Library, Add. MS 32686)

9 Lady Fermanagh, letter from Finmere, 1 October 1711, cited in *The Stoic*, 1928, p.100

10 Geoffrey Webb, ed., *The Complete Works of Sir John Vanbrugh*: IV, *The Letters*, London, 1928, p.112

11 Lord Cobham, letter to his steward, 1714, cited in George Clarke, 'The Vanbrugh-Bridgeman Gardens', The History of Stowe VII, *The Stoic*, XXIII.6, no.139, July 1969, pp.258–9

12 Letter by steward, cited in George Clarke, 'The Vanbrugh-Bridgeman Gardens', The History of Stowe VII, *The Stoic*, XXIII.6, no.139, July 1969, p.258

13 Letter to Daniel Dering, 14 August 1724 (BL, Add. MS 47030, fol.156–9), cited in George Clarke, ed., *Descriptions of Lord Cobham's Gardens at Stowe (1700–1750)*, Buckinghamshire Record Society, no.26, 1990, p.16

14 Ibid., p.15

15 Geoffrey Webb, ed., *The Complete Works of Sir John Vanbrugh*: IV, *The Letters*, London, 1928 p.167

16 'Of Improving the Present Time', 1728 (BL, Add. MS 57804, fol.31), cited in full in George Clarke, ed., *Descriptions of Lord Cobham's Gardens at Stowe (1700–1750)*, Buckinghamshire Record Society, no.26, 1990, pp.25–7

17 Letter to Robert Digby, 12 August [1725], George Sherburn, ed., *The Correspondence of Alexander Pope*, Oxford, 1956, II, p.314

18 Letter to John Knight of Gosfield, August 1731, George Sherburn, ed., *The Correspondence of Alexander Pope*, Oxford, 1956, III, p.217

19 'Elegy XVI. To Mr George Grenville'

20 Paul Whitehead, *Manners: A Satire*, written 1738, lines 128–132, London, 1739, p.10

21 Margaret, Lady Verney, ed., *The Verney Letters of the Eighteenth Century*, London, 1930, II, p.189

22 Letter to Lady Suffolk, Stowe, Sunday morning [1734]; letter to Lady Suffolk, Rousham, 27 June 1734, *Letters to and from Henrietta, Countess of Suffolk, and her second husband, the Hon. George Berkeley, from 1712 to 1767*, London, 1824, II, p.76 and p.79

23 Letter to Martha Blount, 4 July 1739, George Sherburn, ed., *The Correspondence of Alexander Pope*, Oxford, 1956, IV, pp.185–6

24 Southcote, *c*.1752, in James M Osborn, ed., *Joseph Spence: Observations, Anecdotes, and Characters of Books and Men*, Oxford, 1966, I, p.423

25 Letter to Daniel Dering, 14 August 1724 (British Library, Add. MS 47030, fol.156–9), cited in George Clarke, ed., *Descriptions of Lord Cobham's Gardens at Stowe (1700–1750)*, Buckinghamshire Record Society, no.26, 1990, p.16

26 *Letters from … Dr Thomas Herring … to William Duncombe … 1728 to 1757*, London, 1777, pp.39–40

27 *Letterbook of Jemima, Marchioness Grey*, 1748, cited in George Clarke, ed., *Descriptions of Lord Cobham's Gardens at Stowe (1700–1750)*, Buckinghamshire Record Society, no.26, 1990, p.181

28 Letter to the Duchess of Portland, 9 August 1744, Emily J.Climenson, *Elizabeth Montague, Queen of the Bluestockings: Her Correspondence*, London, 1906, I, p.189

29 *The Works of Alexander Pope*, London, 1847, VI, p.408

30 Letter to her brother Lord Carlisle, 20 May 1737. HMC Carlisle, 172, cited in Lord Rosebery, *Chatham: His Early Life and Connections*, London, 1910, p.159

31 Letter dated 14 September, cited in Lord Rosebery, *Lord Chatham: His Early Life and Connections*, London, 1910, p.73

32 Letter dated September 1735 from Lady Suffolk to George Berkeley (BL, Add. MS 22629, fol.43), quoted in Lewis Melville, *Lady Suffolk and her Circle*, London, 1924, p.249

33 Letter from Lady Suffolk to George Berkeley, 2 September 1735 (BL, Add. MS 22629, fol.40), quoted in Lewis Melville, *Lady Suffolk and her Circle*, London, 1924, p.248

34 John Penn, *History and Descriptive Account of Stoke Park*, 1813, cited in Dorothy Stroud, *Capability Brown*, London, 1975, p.48

35 Letter, 24 February 1746/7, found by Mr David Easton in a gardening account in the Huntington Library, cited in George Clarke, 'Lancelot Brown's work at Stowe', The History of Stowe XIV, *The Stoic*, XXV.1, no.146, December 1971, p.21

36 Cited in George Clarke, ed., *Descriptions of Lord Cobham's Gardens at Stowe (1700–1750)*, Buckinghamshire Record Society, no.26, 1990, p.186

37 Cited in Lord Rosebery, *Lord Chatham: His Early Life and Connections*, London, 1910, p.272

38 Letter to George Grenville, 10 November 1748, Huntington Library HM 31555, p.3

39 Letter to George Grenville, [Stowe] 31 December [1748], Huntington Library HM 31557, p.1

4 Earl Temple

40 BL, Add. MS 57,806, fol.76

41 Letter to William Pitt, 4 June 1758, Chatham Papers, National Archives, PRO 30/8/7 pt.2, fol.143

42 *The Travels through England of Dr Richard Pococke*, Camden Society, 1888, I, p.166

43 Birdwood 1994, p.134

44 Letter to William Pitt, Chatham Papers, National Archives. Letter from Earl Temple to William Pitt, 5 August 1755. Quoted in Vere Birdwood, ed., *So dearly loved, so much admired: Letters to Hester Pitt, Lady Chatham*, London, 1994, p.16

45 Ibid.

46 Letter to William Pitt, 17 October [1756], Chatham Papers, National Archives, PRO 30/8/34, fol.144–5. Quoted in Birdwood 1994, p.140

47 Letter to William Pitt, 4 June 1758, Chatham Papers, National Archives, PRO 30/8/7 pt.2, fol.143

48 John Fleming, 'John Adam's Country House Tour II – In Search of Landscape Gardens', *Country Life*, CXXX, 27 July 1961, pp.200–2

49 Letter to Hester Pitt, Stowe, 14 June 1761, Chatham Papers, National Archives, PRO 30/8/62 pt.1, fol.31–34. Quoted in Birdwood 1994, p.18

50 Chatham Papers, National Archives. Quoted in Birdwood 1994, p.18

51 Letter to William Pitt, Stowe, 2 July 1761, Chatham Papers, National Archives, PRO 30/8/7 pt.2, fol.168

52 Letter to Hester Pitt, Stowe, 24 June 1764, Chatham Papers, National Archives, PRO 30/8/62 pt.1, fol.80

53 Stowe Papers, Huntington Library, MO 1335

54 Letter to Wilkes, Stowe, 21 November 1762, in William James Smith, ed., *The Grenville Papers*, London 1852, II, p.4

55 Letter to Countess Chatham, 5 January 1769, Chatham Papers, National Archives, PRO 30/8/62 fol.139. Quoted in Birdwood 1994, p.21

56 Letter to Countess Chatham, 22 July 1762, Chatham Papers, National Archives, PRO 30/8/62 pt.1, fol.44. Cited in Birdwood 1994, p.18

57 Cited in John Martin Robinson, *Temples of Delight*, London, 1990, p.52

58 Vere Birdwood, ed., *So dearly loved, so much admired: Letters to Hester Pitt, Lady Chatham*, London, 1994, pp.12–32

59 Anon., 'Memorandum of the Princess Amelia's visit to Stowe in July, 1764,' in William James Smith, ed., *The Grenville Papers*, London 1852, II, p.408

60 Letter from Gilly Williams to George Selwyn, 30 July 1764, quoted in John Heneage Jesse, *George Selwyn and his Contemporaries*, London, 1843, p.289

61 *Letters and Journals of Lady Mary Coke 1769–71*, 1892, cited in *The Stoic*, July 1932, p.150

62 Cited in George Clarke, 'Earl Temple's Gardens: The First Phase', The History of Stowe XIX, *The Stoic*, XXV.6, no.151, December 1973, pp.265–8

63 Letter to his father, 1st Earl Harcourt, Sudbury, 25 October 1776, *Harcourt Papers*, III, p.123

64 Letter to Hester Pitt, 11 September 1770, Chatham Papers, National Archives, PRO 30/8/34, fol.60

65 Letter to Hester Pitt, Stowe, 8 September 1772. Quoted in Birdwood 1994, p.24

66 Letter to William Pitt, Burton Pynsent, 27 June 1773, Chatham Papers, National Archives, PRO 30/8/9 pt.2, fol.132–3

67 Letter from Earl Temple to Hester Pitt, Stowe, 21 August 1774, Chatham Papers, National Archives, PRO 30/8/63 pt.1, fol.51

68 Letter from Catherine Stapleton to Hester Pitt, Stowe, 2 July 1775, Chatham Papers, National Archives, PRO 30/8/58, fol.181. Quoted in Birdwood 1994, p.193

69 Letter from Lord Nuneham to his father, 1st Earl Harcourt, Sudbury, 25 October 1776, *Harcourt Papers*, III, p.123

70 Letter from George Grenville to his wife, Stowe, 10 April 1777, Huntington Library, STG 47(11) (17th)

71 Letter to William Pitt, Stowe, 28 September 1777, Chatham Papers, National Archives, PRO 30/8/4, fol.473–4

72 Letter from George Grenville to his wife, [11 September 1779], Huntington Library, STG 47(13) III

73 Mrs Paget Toynbee, ed., *The Letters of Horace Walpole*, Oxford, 1903, XI, p.24: letter to the Rev. William Mason, 14 September 1779

5 The first Marquess and the first Duke

74 HMC Fortescue, 1908, I, p.433

75 Betsey, Saturday, 30 December 1797, Anne Fremantle, ed., *The Wynne Diaries*, London, 1940, II, p.198

76 Harriet, Tuesday, 14 February 1804, Anne Fremantle, ed., *The Wynne Diaries*, London, 1940, III, p.107

77 HMC Fortescue, 1908, I, p.78

78 Betsey, Tuesday, 14 January 1808, Anne Fremantle, ed., *The Wynne Diaries*, London, 1940, III, p.316

79 Betsey, Friday, 16 August 1805, Anne Fremantle, ed., *The Wynne Diaries*, London, 1940, III, p.187

80 Ibid, p.188

81 Betsey, Monday, 24 October 1803, Anne Fremantle, ed., *The Wynne Diaries*, London, 1940, III, p.95

82 'A Tour from London to Manchester, Chester, Liverpool and The Lake District', May to July 1831, in Priscilla Boniface, ed., *In Search of English Gardens: The Travels of John Claudius Loudon and his wife Jane*, Wheathampstead, 1987, p.57

83 Prince Hermann von Pückler-Müskau, *Tour in England, Ireland and France in the years 1826, 1827, 1828 and 1829*, Philadelphia, 1833, trans. S Austin, III, p.275

84 *The Gardener's Magazine*, 1831, p.389

6 Decline and fall

85 7 August 1840. *The Letters of Benjamin Disraeli to his Sister 1832 to 1852*, 2004, p.114

86 Royal Archives, A.37.12, quoted in Robert Blake, *Disraeli*, London, 1966, p.494

7 Recovery

87 Noel Annan, *Roxburgh of Stowe*, London, 1965, p.58

88 *The Stoic*, no.132, March 1967

8 The fame of Stowe

89 'Epistle to Burlington', 1731, line 70

90 Cited Osvald Siren, *China and Gardens of Europe in the Eighteenth Century*, 2nd ed., Washington DC, 1990, p.32

91 Thomas Whately, *Observations on Modern Gardening*, London, 1770, p.226

92 Letter from Lord Perceval to Daniel Dering, 14 August 1724 (BL, Add. MSS 47030, ff.156–9). Cited in Clarke 1990, p.15

93 See A.G.Cross, 'By the Banks of the Thames': Russians in Eighteenth-century Britain, Newtonville, Mass., 1980, pp.219–22

Bibliography

Unpublished and visual sources
The Stowe papers in the Henry
E. Huntington Library, San Marino,
California, which include 350,000
documents, provide an unrivalled level
of detailed information on the history
of the garden. Likewise, the visual sources
are more numerous than for any other
English garden. As well as the illustrations
to the guidebooks, amateur drawings and
photographs, two systematic records
were made: the set of 15 views by
Jacques Rigaud, commissioned by Charles
Bridgeman and published in 1739, and
105 wash drawings of the house and gardens
by John Claude Nattes, made in 1805–09.

Guidebooks
The compiler of a modern guide to the
gardens at Stowe must take account of
an exceptionally long tradition, and in
the process add to it. *A Description of the
Gardens of Lord Viscount Cobham at Stow in
Buckinghamshire*, largely based on the
description in the 1742 edition of Daniel
Defoe and Samuel Richardson's *A Tour thro'
the Whole Island of Great Britain*, was published
by Benton Seeley, a writing-master, in 1744.
It was the first guide to a country seat
published in England for the general reader
or tourist, and found a ready market. New
editions were printed in successive years
until 1749, and Seeley brought out two
'companion' volumes, William Gilpin's
A Dialogue upon the Gardens at Stow and a set
of *Views of the Temples and other Ornamental
Buildings in the Gardens at Stow* in 1748 and
1750. In the latter year the topographical
engraver George Bickham published in
London *The Beauties of Stow*, a pirated
conflation of all three of Seeley's books,
with new illustrations. Competition led
both publishers towards wider distribution
and further refinements, such as maps.
Eventually Seeley prevailed and his guides
continued to be printed until 1827. In the
twentieth century the tradition was extended
by Laurence Whistler, Michael Gibbon,
and George Clarke's *Stowe: A Guide to the
Gardens*, first published in 1956 and revised
in 1968 and 1974. For the bibliography of
the early guides, see John Harris's *A Country
House Index* (1977) and Clarke's introduction
to the 1977 facsimile of Bickham's *The
Beauties of Stow*.

ADDISON, JOSEPH, 'A Continuation of the
Vision', *The Tatler*, no.123, 21 January 1709

ANNAN, NOEL, *Roxburgh of Stowe*, London,
1965

BECKETT, JOHN V., *The Rise and Fall of the
Grenvilles*, Manchester, 1994

BEVINGTON, MICHAEL, 'The Development of
the Classical Revival at Stowe', *Architectura*,
XXI, no.2, 1991, pp.136–63
—— *Templa Quam Dilecta*, nos 1–13, 1989
—— *Stowe: A Guide to the House*, Stowe,
1990
—— *Stowe: The Garden and Park*, 3rd ed.,
Stowe, 1996

BIRDWOOD, VERE, ed., *So dearly loved, so much
admired: Letters to Hester Pitt, Lady Chatham ...*,
London, 1994

BOYSE, SAMUEL, 'The Triumphs of Nature:
A Poem on the Magnificent Gardens at
Stowe in Buckinghamshire, the Seat of the
Rt. Hon. Lord Cobham', *Gentleman's
Magazine*, XII, June 1742, p.234, July,
pp.380–2, August, pp.435–6 (repr. in
Clarke 1990, pp.94–100)

BRIDGEMAN, SARAH, *General Plan of the Woods,
Park and Gardens of Stowe, with Several
Perspective Views in the Garden*, Thomas
Bowles, 1746

BUCKINGHAM AND CHANDOS, Richard
Temple-Nugent-Brydges-Chandos-Grenville,
1st Duke of, *Private Diary*, I–III, Hurst and
Blackett, 1862

BURRELL, MICHAEL AND INNIS, *The Temple of
British Worthies: An Illustrated Guide*, 1983

CHATELAIN, J.B., *Sixteen Perspective Views,
together with a General Plan of the ... Buildings
and Gardens at Stowe ... drawn on the Spot 1752*,
engraved by George Bickham junior, 1752

CHRISTIE & MANSON, *Catalogue of the Contents
of Stowe, near Buckingham (Seat of the Duke of
Buckingham & Chandos) which will be sold by
auction by Messrs Christie & Manson*, William
Clowes [1848]

CLARKE, GEORGE B., and GIBBON, MICHAEL
J., 'The History of Stowe', *The Stoic*, I–XXVI,
1967–77

CLARKE, GEORGE B., 'The Early Gardens at
Stowe (for Sir Richard Temple, 1679–1697)',
Country Life, CXLV, 2 January 1969, pp.6–9
—— 'Military Gardening at Stowe',
Country Life, CLI, 18 May 1972, pp.1254–6
—— 'William Kent, Heresy in Stowe's
Elysium', in Peter Willis, ed., *Furor Hortensis*,
1973, pp.48–56

—— 'The Gardens of Stowe', *Apollo*, XCVII, June 1973, pp.558–65
—— 'Grecian Taste and Gothic Virtue: Lord Cobham's Gardening Programme and its Iconography', *Apollo*, XCVI, June 1973, pp.566–71
—— 'The Medallions of Concord: An Association between the Society of Arts and Stowe', *Journal of the Royal Society of Arts*, CXXIX, August 1981, pp.611–16
—— 'Where did all the Trees come from? An Analysis of Bridgeman's Planting at Stowe', *Journal of Garden History*, v, January/March 1985, pp.72–83
—— 'Signor Fido and the Stowe Patriots', *Apollo*, CXXII, October 1985, pp.248–51
—— ed., 'Descriptions of Lord Cobham's Gardens at Stowe, 1700–1750', *Buckinghamshire Record Society*, 1990
—— 'The Moving Temples of Stowe: Aesthetics of Change in an English Landscape over Four Generations', *Huntington Library Quarterly*, LV, 1992, pp.479–532

CORNFORTH, JOHN, 'Achievement and Challenge: The Preservation of the Stowe Landscape', *Country Life*, CLXXIX, 24 April 1986, pp.1108–10

CREIGHTON, HUGH, 'Repairs to the Garden Buildings at Stowe', *The Stoic*, March 1967, p.206

FITZGERALD, DESMOND, 'History of the Interior of Stowe', *Apollo*, LXXVII, June 1973, pp.572–85

FORSTER, HENRY RUMSEY, ed., *The Stowe Catalogue priced and annotated … sale … entrusted to Messrs Christie and Manson etc.*, David Bogue, 1848

GIBBON, MICHAEL J., 'A Forgotten Italian at Stowe: Vincenzo Valdrè, Architect and Painter', *Country Life*, CXL, 4 August 1966, pp.260–3
—— 'The Queen's Temple at Stowe', *Country Life*, CXLV, 9 January 1969, pp.78–80
—— 'Manifesto in Ironstone: The Gothic Temple at Stowe', *Country Life*, CLI, 1 June 1972, pp.1416–17
—— 'Stowe House, 1680–1779', *Apollo*, XCVII, June 1973, pp.552–7
—— 'The First Neo-classical Building? Temple of Concord, Stowe', *Country Life*, CLV, 11 April 1974, pp.852–3
—— 'Stowe, Buckinghamshire: The House and Garden Buildings and their Designers: A Catalogue', *Architectural History*, XX, 1977, pp.31–44; with George Clarke, 'Addenda to Stowe', XXI, 1978, p.93

HALL, MICHAEL, 'Stowe Landscape Gardens I & II', *Country Life*, 22, 29 February 1996

HARRIS, JOHN, 'Blondel at Stowe', *Connoisseur*, CLV, March 1964, pp.173–6

HAYDEN, PETER, 'British Seats on Imperial Russian Tables', *Garden History*, XIII, no.1, 1985, pp.17–32
—— 'The Russian Stowe: Benton Seeley's Guidebooks as a Source of Catherine the Great's Park at Tsarskoe Selo', *Garden History*, XIX, no.1, spring 1991, pp.21–7

HUSSEY, CHRISTOPHER, 'Stowe, Buckinghamshire: 1. The Connection of Georgian Landscape with Whig Politics', *Country Life*, CII, 12 September 1947, pp.526–9; '2 Rhetoric in Landscape Architecture', 19 September 1947, pp.578–81; '3. Heroic Phase', 26 September 1947, pp.626–9
—— *English Landscape Gardens*, 1967, pp.89–113

INSKIP, PETER, 'Discoveries, Challenges and Moral Dilemmas in the Restoration of the Garden Buildings at Stowe', *Huntington Library Quarterly*, LV, 1992, pp.511–26

JACKSON-STOPS (Auctioneers), *The Ducal Estate at Stowe*, Towcester, 1921, 1922

JACKSON-STOPS, GERVASE, *An English Arcadia 1600–1990*, 1991
—— 'Sharawadgi Rediscovered: The Chinese House at Stowe', *Apollo*, CXXXVII, no.374, April 1993, pp.217–22

KENWORTHY-BROWNE, JOHN, 'Rysbrack's Saxon Deities', *Apollo*, CXXII, September 1985, pp.220–7

LIPSCOMB, GEORGE, *The History and Antiquities of the County of Buckingham*, III, 1843, pp.84–108

MCCARTHY, MICHAEL, 'Eighteenth Century Amateur Architects and their Gardens', in Nikolaus Pevsner, ed., *The Picturesque Garden & its Influence outside the British Isles*, pp.31–55
—— 'James Lovell and his Sculptures at Stowe', *Burlington Magazine*, CXV, no.841, April 1973, pp.221–32
—— 'The Rebuilding of Stowe House, 1770–1777', *Huntington Library Quarterly*, XXXVI, no.3, 1973, pp.267–89

MOORE, SUSAN, 'Hail! Gods of our Forefathers: Rysbrack's "Lost" Saxon Deities at Stowe', *Country Life*, 31 January 1985

ROBINSON, JOHN MARTIN, *Temples of Delight: Stowe Landscape Gardens*, 1990

SHEAHAN, JAMES JOSEPH, *History and Topography of Buckinghamshire*, 1862

THOMPSON, F.M.L., 'The end of a great estate', *Economic History Review*, 2nd ser., VIII, 1 August 1955, pp.36–52

WEST, GILBERT, *Stowe*, 1732 (repr. in Clarke, 1990, pp.36–51)

WHATELY, THOMAS, *Observations on Modern Gardening*, Dublin, 1770

WHEELER, RICHARD W., 'The Park and Garden Survey at Stowe: The Replanting and Restoration of the Historical Landscape', *Huntington Library Quarterly*, LV, 1992, pp.527–32
—— 'The Gardens of Stowe and West Wycombe: Paradise and Parody?', *Apollo*, CXLV, April 1997, pp.3–7

WHISTLER, LAURENCE, 'The Authorship of Stowe Temples', *Country Life*, CVIII, 29 September 1950, pp.1002–6
—— *The Imagination of Vanbrugh and his Fellow Artists*, 1954
—— 'Signor Borra at Stowe', *Country Life*, CXXII, 29 August 1957, pp.390–3
—— *Stowe: A Guide to the Gardens*, 1956, 2nd rev.ed. by Laurence Whistler, Michael Gibbon and George Clarke, Buckingham, 1968; 3rd rev.ed. 1974

WHITE, T.H., *Mistress Masham's Repose*, London, 1947

WHITFIELD, PAUL, 'Bankruptcy and Sale at Stowe: 1848', *Apollo*, XCVII, June 1973, pp.599–604

WHITWELL, STEPHEN, 'Expelled to Stowe: the Comte de Paris in Exile', *Country Life*, CLXXXIII, 7 December 1989, pp.180–6

WILLIAMS-ELLIS, CLOUGH, 'Stowe, Past and Future', *The Spectator*, CXXVII, 23 July 1921, p.103

WILLIS, PETER, 'From Desert to Eden: Charles Bridgeman's "Capital Stroke"', *Burlington Magazine*, CXV, no.840, March 1973, pp.150–7
—— *Charles Bridgeman and the English Landscape Garden*, 1977, pp.106–27

WOODBRIDGE, KENNETH, 'William Kent as Landscape Gardener: A Re-appraisal', *Apollo*, C, 1974, pp.126–37

Index

Figures in **bold** indicate captions.